"Comrade—both a nom de guerre and a sign of love. One which constructs political organization and struggle, and which brings back from the grave the fallen heroes."

—Antonio Negri, co-author *of Empire*

"I can't shut up about *Comrade*, a brilliant and hopeful book. In its sharp critique of neoliberalism's creepy capture of left politics and relations, Jodi Dean points the way forward with clarity, humor and joy. This is the book that the left urgently needs right now, and I can't wait to make everyone read it."

—Liza Featherstone, author of *Selling Women Short*

"In this era of hashtag politics, branding, and call out culture, when 'identity politics' functions more like enclosure than grounds for solidarity, when planetary annihilation is deemed inevitable and racism permanent, Jodi Dean recovers the keyword absent from our radical vocabulary: comrade. Her guided tour through communist histories reveals the power of comrade as a form of revolutionary belonging, a mode of address, a great equalizer, and an expression of disciplined and committed love distinct from eros, philia, and agape. Read *Comrade*. Be Comrades!"

—Robin D. G. Kelley, author of *Freedom Dreams: The Black Radical Tradition*

"Rarely has the notion of 'comrade', symbolic, imaginary and concrete, been more needed  this vivid, elegant ...Dean ...sent ...ty for ...es ...litical ...ssential reading for all those committed to a politics of hope in any inclusive emancipatory and egalitarian struggles."

—Lynne Segal, author of *Radical Happiness: Moments of Collective Joy*

"Part speculative conceptual history and part militant political theory continuing in the same vein as her previous publications *The Communist Horizon* and *Crowds and Party*, this new book on the generic figure of the comrade as a form of address, an index of belonging, and a carrier of expectations presents Jodi Dean at her very best: witty from beginning to end, scathing as need be against those who would prefer to hamper, mock, or red-bait the prospects of egalitarian communist and socialist politics, and never less than urgently needed as a program for common struggle in these times of renewed authoritarianism, unabashed sexism, and emboldened racism."

—Bruno Bosteels, author of *The Actuality of Communism*

COMRADE

COMRADE

An Essay on Political Belonging

Jodi Dean

VERSO
London • New York

First published by Verso 2019
© Jodi Dean 2019

3 5 7 9 10 8 6 4 2

Verso
UK: 6 Meard Street, London W1F 0EG
US: 20 Jay Street, Suite 1010, Brooklyn, NY 11201
versobooks.com

Verso is the imprint of New Left Books

ISBN-13: 978-1-78873-501-8
ISBN-13: 978-1-78873-503-2 (UK EBK)
ISBN-13: 978-1-78873-504-9 (US EBK)

British Library Cataloguing in Publication Data
A catalogue record for this book is available from the British Library

Library of Congress Cataloging-in-Publication Data
A catalog record for this book is available from the Library of Congress

Typeset in Garamond by Biblichor Ltd, Edinburgh
Printed and bound by CPI Group (UK) Ltd, Croydon CR0 4YY

Dedicated to M. F.

Contents

Contents

Acknowledgements

The weight of acknowledging the many people who contributed to this book is nearly too much to bear. Every word draws from lessons learned from working with others, not all of whom I know by name. I am especially grateful for the challenging support of the directors and participants in the annual meeting of the Radical Critical Theory Circle in Nisyros, Greece; for the generosity of colleagues who have provided me with opportunities to present portions of the book in public lectures and seminars; and to the militant organizers of the Geneva Women's Assembly for what they teach me every day. I want to extend special thanks to Paul Apostolidis, Maria Aristodemou, Bernard Aspe, Albena Azmanova, Darin Barney, Paul Buhle, Maria Chehonadskih, Carl Davidson, Alla Ivanchikova, Andreas Kalyvas, Kian Kenyon-Dean, Regina Kreide, Rob Maclean, Artemy Magun, James Martel, Korinna Patelis, Alexei Penzin, Kenneth Reinhard, David Riff, Corey Robin, Marcela Romero-Rivera, Laura Salamendra, Christian Sorace, and Oxana Timofeeva. I am grateful to Hannah Dickinson, Kai Heron, and Sadie Kenyon-Dean, as well as my editor, Rosie Warren, for their comments on the manuscript. As always, I am appreciative beyond measure for the patience and love of my partner, Paul Passavant.

CHAPTER ONE

From Allies to Comrades

SEVERAL JOKES IN PRESIDENT Barack Obama's address at the 2016 White House Correspondents' Dinner targeted Senator Bernie Sanders. Sanders was running a surprisingly strong campaign against the Democratic Party's presumptive presidential nominee, former secretary of state Hillary Clinton. After a few shoutouts to celebrities and politicians, Obama turned to the subject of Sanders, saying:

A lot of folks have been surprised by the Bernie phenomenon, especially his appeal to young people. But not me, I get it. Just recently, a young person came up to me and said she was sick of politicians standing in the way of her dreams. As if we were actually going to let Malia go to Burning Man this year. (Laughter.) That was not going to happen. (Laughter.) Bernie might have let her go. (Laughter.) Not us. (Laughter.)

I am hurt, though, Bernie, that you're distancing yourself a little from me. (Laughter.) I mean, that's just not something that you do to your comrade. (Laughter and applause.)[1]

The last joke points to the socialist opening Sanders's campaign cut into US politics. At first glance, the joke seems like red-baiting—Obama's thinly veiled reminder that Sanders was a self-identified socialist and thus unacceptable to the US political class. But perhaps not. Maybe it was a reminder for the audience that Sanders wasn't a member of the Democratic Party, and so he wasn't Obama's party comrade at all. Sanders wanted the Democratic nomination for president but he wasn't actually a Democrat. There is also a third way of reading the joke. Recall how persistently the US right red-baited Obama, accusing him of being a communist or socialist. For eight years, the right excoriated the country's first black president as the most radical left-wing official ever to inhabit the White House. Mocking "Comrade Obama," the right associated Obama with Lenin and Stalin, Che and Mao. Read this way, the joke points not to *Sanders* as a comrade but to *Obama* as a comrade. Obama could have been referring to himself as Sanders's comrade, as someone who shares with Sanders a common political horizon, the emancipatory egalitarian horizon denoted by the term comrade. If they were on the same side, with Obama being Sanders's comrade, then Obama should have been able to expect a little solidarity. The joke worked because everybody in the room—from celebrities, to Washington insiders, to media moguls—knew full well that Obama wasn't a comrade. He doesn't come close to sharing Sanders's politics, even if the right can't tell the difference between them.

The term *comrade* indexes a political relation, a set of expectations for action toward a common goal. It highlights the sameness of those on the same side—no matter their differences, comrades stand together. As Obama's joke implies, when you share a politics, you don't generally distance yourself from your comrades. Comradeship binds action, and in this binding, this solidarity, it collectivizes and directs action in light of a shared vision for the future. For communists, this is the egalitarian future of a society emancipated from the determinations of private property and capitalism and reorganized according to the free association, common benefit, and collective decisions of the producers.

But the term comrade predates its use by communists and socialists. In romance languages, comrade first appears in the sixteenth century to designate one who shares a room with another. Juan A. Herrero Brasas cites a Spanish historical-linguistic dictionary's definition of the term: "*Camarada* is someone who is so close to another man that he eats and sleeps in the same house with him."[2] In French, the term was originally feminine, *camarade*, and referred to a barracks or room shared by soldiers.[3] Etymologically, comrade derives from *camera*, the Latin word for room, chamber, and vault. The technical connotation of *vault* indexes a generic function, the structure that produces a particular space and holds it open.[4] A chamber or room is a repeatable structure that takes its form by producing an inside separate from an outside and providing a supported cover for those underneath it. Sharing a room, sharing a space, generates a closeness, an intensity of feeling and expectation of solidarity that differentiates those on one side from those on the other. Comradeship is a political relation of supported cover.

Interested in comrade as a mode of address, carrier of expectations, and figure of belonging in the communist and socialist traditions, I emphasize the comrade as a generic figure for the political relation between those on the same side of a political struggle. Comrades are those who tie themselves together instrumentally, for a common purpose: *If we want to win—and we have to win—we must act together.* As Angela Davis describes her decision to join the Communist Party:

> I wanted an anchor, a base, a mooring. I needed comrades with whom I could share a common ideology. I was tired of ephemeral ad-hoc groups that fell apart when faced with the slightest difficulty; tired of men who measured their sexual height by women's intellectual genuflection. It wasn't that I was fearless,

but I knew that to win, we had to fight and the fight that would win was the one collectively waged by the masses of our people and working people in general. I knew that this fight had to be led by a group, a party with more permanence in its membership and structure and substance in its ideology.[5]

Comrades are those you can count on. You share enough of a common ideology, enough of a commitment to common principles and goals, to do more than one-off actions. Together you can fight the long fight.

As comrades, our actions are voluntary, but they are not always of our own choosing. Comrades have to be able to count on each other even when we don't like each other and even when we disagree. We do what needs to be done because we owe it to our comrades. In *The Romance of American Communism*, Vivian Gornick reports the words of a former member of the Communist Party USA, or CPUSA, who hated the daily grind of selling papers and canvassing expected of party cadre, but nevertheless, according to her, "I did it. I did it because if I didn't do it, I couldn't face my comrades the next day. And we all did it for the same reason: we were accountable to each other."[6] Put in psychoanalytic terms, the comrade functions as an ego ideal: the point from which party members assess themselves as doing important, meaningful work.[7] Being accountable to another entails seeing your actions through their eyes. Are you letting them down or are you doing work that they respect and admire?

In *Crowds and Party*, I present the good comrade as an ideal ego, that is to say, as how party members imagine themselves.[8] They may imagine themselves as thrilling orators, brilliant polemicists, skilled organizers, or courageous militants. In contrast with my discussion there, in the current book, I draw out how the comrade also functions as an ego ideal, the perspective that party members—and often fellow travelers—take toward themselves. This perspective is the effect of belonging on the same side as it works back on those who have committed themselves to common struggle. The comrade is a symbolic as well as an imaginary figure and it is the symbolic dimension of ego ideal I focus on here.

My thinking about the comrade as a generic figure for those on the same side flows out of my work on communism as the horizon of left politics and my work on the party as the political form necessary for this politics.[9] To see our political horizon as communist is to highlight the emancipatory egalitarian struggle of the proletarianized against capitalist exploitation—that is, against the determination of life by market forces; by value; by the division of labor (on the basis of sex and race); by imperialism (theorized by Lenin in terms of the dominance of monopoly and finance capital); and by neocolonialism (theorized by Nkrumah as the last stage of imperialism). Today we see this horizon in struggles such as those led by women of color against police violence, white supremacy, and the murder and incarceration of black, brown, and working-class people. We see it in the infrastructure battles around pipelines, climate justice, and barely habitable cities with undrinkable water and contaminated soil. We see it in the array of social reproduction struggles against debt, foreclosure, and privatization, and for free, quality public housing, childcare, education, transportation, healthcare, and other basic services. We see it in the ongoing fight of LGBTQ people against harassment, discrimination, and oppression.

It is readily apparent today that the communist horizon is the horizon of political struggle not for the nation but for the world; it is an international horizon. This is evident in the antagonism between the rights of immigrants and refugees and intensified nationalisms; in the necessity of a global response to planetary warming; and in anti-imperialist, decolonization, and peace movements. In these examples, communism is a force of negativity, the negation of the global capitalist present.

Communism is also the name for the positive alternative to capitalism's permanent and expanding exploitation, crisis, and

immiseration, the name of a system of production based on meeting social needs—*from each according to ability to each according
to need*, to paraphrase Marx's famous slogan—in a way that is
collectively determined and carried out by the producers. This
positive dimension of communism attends to social relations, to
how people treat each other, animals, things, and the world
around them. Building communism entails more than resistance
and riot. It requires the emancipated egalitarian organization of
collective life.

With respect to the party, intellectuals on the contemporary
left tend to extract the party from the aspirations and accomplish-
ments it enabled. Communist philosophers who disagree on a slew
of theoretical questions, such as Antonio Negri and Alain Badiou,
converge on the organizational question—no party! The party has
been rejected as authoritarian, as outmoded, as ill-fitting a society
of networks. Every other mode of political association may be
revised, renewed, rethought, or reimagined except for the party of
communists.

This rejection of the party as a form for left politics is a mistake.
It ignores the effects of association on those engaged in common
struggle. It fails to learn from the everyday experiences of generations of activists, organizers, and revolutionaries. It relies on a
narrow, fantasied notion of the party as a totalitarian machine. It
neglects the courage, enthusiasm, and achievements of millions of
party members for over a century. Rejection of the party form has
been left dogmatism for the last thirty years and has gotten us
nowhere.

Fortunately, the movements of the squares in Greece and Spain,
as well as lessons from the successes and limits of the Occupy
movement, have pushed against this left dogmatism. They have
reenergized interest in the party as a political form that can scale;
a form that is flexible, adaptive, and expansive enough to endure
beyond the joyous and disruptive moments of crowds in the streets.
A theory of the comrade contributes to this renewal by drawing

out the ways that shared commitment to a common struggle generates new strengths and new capacities. Over and against the reduction of party relations to the relations between the leaders and the led, comrade attends to the effects of political belonging on those on the same side of a political struggle. As we fight together for a world free of exploitation, oppression, and bigotry, we have to be able to trust and count on each other. Comrade names this relation.

The comrade relation remakes the place from which one sees, what it is possible to see, and what possibilities can appear. It enables the revaluation of work and time, what one does, and for whom one does it. Is one's work done for the people or for the bosses? Is it voluntary or done because one has to work? Does one work for personal provisions or for a collective good? We should recall Marx's lyrical description of communism in which work becomes "life's prime want." We get a glimpse of that in comradeship: one *wants* to do political work. You don't want to let down your comrades; you see the value of your work through their eyes, your new collective eyes. Work, determined not by markets but by shared commitments, becomes fulfilling. French communist philosopher and militant Bernard Aspe discusses the problem of contemporary capitalism as a loss of "common time"; that is, the loss of an experience of time generated and enjoyed through our collective being-together.[10] From holidays, to meals, to breaks, whatever common time we have is synchronized and enclosed in forms for capitalist appropriation. Communicative capitalism's apps and trackers amplify this process such that the time of consumption can be measured in much the same way that Taylorism measured the time of production: How long did a viewer spend on a particular web page? Did a person watch a whole ad or click off of it after five seconds? In contrast, the common action that is the actuality of communist movement induces a collective change in capacities. Breaking from capitalism's 24-7 injunctions to produce and consume for the bosses and owners, the discipline of common struggle expands possibilities for action and intensifies the sense of its necessity. The comrade is a figure for the relation through which this transformation of work and time occurs.

How do we imagine political work? Under conditions where political change seems completely out of reach, we might imagine political work as self-transformation. At the very least, we can work on ourselves. In the intensely mediated networks of communicative capitalism, we might see our social media engagements as a kind of activism where Twitter and Facebook function as important sites of struggle. Perhaps we understand writing as important political work and hammer out opinion pieces, letters to the editors, and manifestoes. When we imagine political work, we often take electoral politics as our frame of reference, focusing on voting, lawn signs, bumper stickers, and campaign buttons. Or we think of activists as those who arrange phone banks, canvass door-to-door, and set up rallies. In yet another political imaginary, we might envision political work as study, whether done alone or with others. We might imagine political work as cultural production, the building of new communities, spaces, and ways of seeing. Our imaginary might have a militant, or even militarist, inflection: political work is carried out through marches, occupations, strikes, and blockades; through civil disobedience, direct action, and covert operations. Even with the recognition of the wide array of political activities, the ways people use them to respond to specific situations and capacities, and how they combine to enhance each other, we might still imagine radical political work as punching a Nazi in the face.

Throughout these various actions and activities, how are the relations among those fighting on the same side imagined? How do the activists and organizers, militants and revolutionaries relate to one another? During the weeks and months when the Occupy movement was at its peak, relations with others were often infused with a joyous sense of being together, with an enthusiasm for the collective co-creation of new patterns of action and ways of living.[11] But the feeling didn't last. The pressures of organizing diverse people and politics under conditions of police repression and real material need wore down even the most committed activists. Since then, on social media and across the broader left, relations among the politically engaged have again become tense and conflicted, often along lines of race and gender. Dispersed and disorganized, we're uncertain of whom to trust and what to expect. We encounter contradictory injunctions to self-care and call out. Suspicion undermines support. Exhaustion displaces enthusiasm.

Attention to comradeship, to the ways that shared expectations make political work not just possible but also gratifying, may help redirect our energies back to our common struggle. As former CPUSA member David Ross explained to Gornick:

> I knew that I could never feel passionately about the new movements as I had about the old, I realized that the CP has provided me with a sense of comradeship I would never have again, and that without that comradeship I could *never* be political.[12]

For Ross, the Communist Party is what made Marxism. The party gave Marxism life, political purpose. This life-giving capacity came from comradeship. Ross continues: "The idea of politics as simply a diffused consciousness linked only to personal integrity was— *is*—anathema to me." His description of politics as "a diffused consciousness linked only to personal integrity" fits today's left milieus. Perhaps, then, his remedy—comradeship—will as well.

Various people have told me their stories of feeling a rush of warmth when they were first welcomed into their party as a comrade. I've had this feeling myself. In his memoir *Incognegro: A Memoir of Exile and Apartheid*, the theorist Frank Wilderson, a former member of uMkhonto weSizwe, or MK, the armed wing of the African National Congress (ANC), describes his first meeting with Chris Hani, the leader of the South African Communist

Party and the chief of staff of MK. Wilderson writes, "I beamed like a schoolboy when he called me 'comrade.'"[13] Wilderson chides himself for what he calls a "childish need for recognition."[14] Perhaps because he still puts Hani on a pedestal, he feels exposed in his enjoyment of the egalitarian disruption of comradeship. Wilderson hasn't yet internalized the idea that he and Hani are political equals. "Comrade" holds out an equalizing promise, and when that promise is fulfilled, we confront our own continuing yet unwanted attachments to hierarchy, prestige, inadequacy. Accepting equality takes courage.

Wilderson's joy in hearing Hani call him "comrade" contrasts sharply with another instance Wilderson recounts where comrade was the term of address. In 1994, shortly before Wilderson was forced to leave South Africa, he encountered Nelson Mandela at an event hosted by *Tribute* magazine. After Mandela's public remarks, Wilderson asked a question in which he addressed Mandela as "comrade." "Not Mr. Mandela. Not sir, like the fawning advertising mogul who asked the first question. Comrade Mandela. It stitched him back into the militant garb he'd shed since the day he left prison."[15] Wilderson's recollection shows how comrade's equalizing insistence can be aggressive, an imposition of discipline. This is part of its power. Addressing another as "comrade" reminds them that something is expected of them.

Discipline and joy are two sides of the same coin, two aspects of comradeship as a mode of political belonging. As a form of address, figure of political relation, and carrier of expectations, comrade disrupts capitalist society's hierarchical identifications of sex, race, and class. It insists on the equalizing sameness of those on the same side of a political struggle and renders that equalizing sameness productive of new modes of work and belonging. In this respect, comrade is a carrier of utopian longings in the sense theorized by Kathi Weeks. Weeks presents the utopian form as carrying out two functions: "One function is to alter our connection to the present, while the other is to shift our relationship to the future;

one is productive of estrangement, the other of hope."[16] The first function mobilizes the negativity of disidentification and disinvestment. Present relations become strange, less binding on our sense of possibility. The second function redirects "our attention and energies toward an open future . . . providing a vision or glimmer of a better world."[17] The power of comrade is in how it negates old relations and promises new ones—the promise itself ushers them in, welcoming the new comrade into relations irreducible to their broader setting.

Survivors and Systems

This book offers a theory of the comrade as a figure for the political relation between those on the same side. It contrasts with two opposing tendencies dominant in contemporary left theory and activism, tendencies that emphasize survivors and systems. The emphasis on survivors appears in social media, academic environments, and some activist networks. It is voiced through intense attachment to identity and appeals to allyship, as I explore below. The emphasis on systems predominates in aesthetic and conceptual venues as a posthumanist concern with geology, extinction, algorithms, "hyperobjects," biosystems, and planetary exhaustion.[18] So on the one side, we have survivors, those with nothing left to cling to but their identities, often identities forged through struggles to survive and attached to the pain and trauma of these struggles.[19] And on the other, we have systems, processes operating at a scale so vast, so complex, that we can scarcely conceive of them, let alone affect them.[20] This book presents an alternative to both.

These two tendencies correspond to neoliberal capitalism's dismantling of social institutions, and to the intensification of capitalism via networked, personalized digital media and informatization that I call "communicative capitalism."[21] More and more people are experiencing more and more economic uncertainty, insecurity, and instability. Good jobs are harder to find and easier to lose. Fewer people can count on long-term employment, or expect that benefits like quality healthcare and adequate provision for retirement will be part of their compensation. Unions are smaller and weaker. Wages are stagnant. Housing is unaffordable and inadequate. Schools and universities face cuts to budgets and faculty, additions of administrators and students, astronomical tuition increases, more debt, and less respect. Pummeled by competition, debt, and the general dismantling of the remnants of public and infrastructural supports, families crumble. Neoliberal ideology glosses the situation as one where individuals have more choice and more opportunity to exercise personal responsibility.

Carl Schmitt famously characterized liberalism as replacing politics with ethics and economics.[22] Correlatively, we should note the displacement of politics specific to neoliberalism. There is individualized self-cultivation, self-management, self-reliance, self-absorption, and—at the same time—impersonal determining processes, circuits, and systems. We have responsible individuals, individuals who are responsibilized, treated as loci of autonomous choices and decisions, and we have individuals encountering situations that are utterly determining and outside their control. Instead of ethics and economics, neoliberalism's displacement of politics manifests in the opposition between survivors and systems. The former struggle to persist in conditions of unlivability rather than to seize and transform these conditions. The latter are systems and "hyperobjects" determining us, often aesthetic objects or objects of a future aesthetics, things to view and diagram and predict and perhaps even mourn, but not to affect.[23]

Survivors experience their vulnerability. Some even come to cherish it, to derive their sense of self from being able to survive against all that is stacked against them. Sociologist Jennifer Silva interviewed a number of working-class young adults in Massachusetts and Virginia.[24] Many emphasized their self-reliance. They did so in part because their experience told them that other people were likely to continue to fail or betray them. To survive, they could count only on themselves. Some of the people described struggles with illness, battles with addiction, and challenges with overcoming dysfunctional families and abusive relationships. For them, the fight to survive is the key feature of an identity imagined as dignified and heroic because it has to produce itself by itself.

Accounts of systems are typically devoid of survivors.[25] Human lives don't matter. The presumption that they matter is taken to be an epistemological failure or ontological crime in need of remedy. Bacteria and rocks, planetary or even galactic processes, are what need to be taken into account, brought in to redirect thought away from anthropocentric hubris. When people appear, they are the problem, a planetary excess that needs to be curtailed, a destructive species run amok, the glitch of life.

The opposition between survivors and systems gives us a left devoid of politics. Both tendencies render class struggle—the divisive struggle over common conditions on behalf of an emancipatory egalitarian future—unintelligible. In the place of the political struggle of the proletarianized, we have the fragmenting assertion of particularity, of unique survival, and an obsession with the encroaching, unavoidable impossibility of survival. Politics is effaced in the impasse of individualized survivability under conditions of generalized non-survival, of extinction.

However strong the survivors and systems tendencies may be on the contemporary left, our present setting still provides openings for politics. Here are four. First, communicative capitalism is marked by the power of many, of number. Capitalist and state power emphasizes big data and the knowledge generated by finding correlations in enormous data sets. Social media is driven by the power of number: how many friends and followers, how many shares and retweets? On the streets and in the movements, we see further emphasis on number—the many who are rioting, demonstrating, occupying, blockading. As over a century of working-class struggle has demonstrated, the power of the people is in asserting the power that the many have over the few—if the people can get organized and join together enough to take the struggle on. A second opening exists in identity losing its ability to ground a left politics. No political conclusions follow from the assertion of a specific identity. On the left, attributions of identity are being immediately complicated, critiqued, and even rejected as activists build commonalities across struggles. Advancing nationalisms throughout the world suggest that today identity is more likely to be appealed to by the right. Yet again, the right repeats its age-old tactic of stealing left themes and programs, now forwarding an identity politics of its own: white supremacy in the United States, Brexit in the UK, Hindu nationalism, and Israel's declaration that it is the nation-state of the Jewish people are but a few examples. The third opening relates to the astronomical increase in demands on our attention that circulate in communicative capitalism, for which a series of communicative shortcuts have emerged: hashtags, memes, emojis, and reaction GIFs, as well as linguistic patterns optimized for search engines (lists, questions, indicators, hooks, and lures).[26] These shortcuts point to the prominence of generic markers—common images and symbols that facilitate communicative flow, keeping circulation fluid. If we had to read, much less think about, everything we share online, our social media networks would slow down and clog up. In this setting, the generic serves as a container for multiplicities of incommunicable contents. Common symbols enable new connections between struggles; common names let people understand their local issues as instances of something larger, something global. In the fourth opening, the movements themselves have come up against the limits of horizontality, individuality, and rhetorics of allyship that presuppose fixed identities and interests. The response has been renewed interest in the politics of parties and questions of the party form, renewed emphasis on organizing the proletarianized many. Cutting through and across the impasse of survivor and system is a new turn toward the arrangements of the many, the institutions of the common, and the struggles of the exploited.[27]

This is the context in which I present a theory of the comrade. The comrade figures a political relation that shifts us away from preoccupations with survivors and systems, away from the suppositions of unique particularity and the impossibility of politics, and toward the sameness of those fighting on the same side. It draws out the demands on and expectations of those engaged in emancipatory egalitarian political struggle. Comradeship engenders discipline, joy, courage, and enthusiasm, as I explore further in chapter three. If the left is as committed to radical change as we claim, we have to be comrades.

From Allies to Comrades

For some contemporary readers, comrade as a term of address might seem jarring, out of place. In the United States, perhaps the term is too alien to American political culture. In Europe, the term might seem too Stalinist, too old school, and too restrictive. Terms like "colleague," implying less commitment and fitting more easily into the European Union's capitalist setting, may be more commonly used and feel more comfortable. These views are not entirely without merit.

The US-based hesitation nevertheless ignores the history of socialism and communism in the United States. And the broader hesitation needs to be associated with the defeat of the Soviet Union, intense neoliberalization, and capitalist ideology's cult of individual identity. In a context theorized as post-political and postdemocratic, the personal—what the individual experiences, feels, and risks—has turned into the privileged site of political engagement. Given neoliberalism's subjection of public and political practices and institutions to market demands this is not surprising. But what the left has claimed as a victory is the symptom of its defeat: the erosion of working-class political power and the accompanying decay of its political parties. The claim that the term comrade doesn't ring true is thus more symptomatic than it is descriptive. It attests to a situation that has to be changed, a problem that needs to be solved, and an organization that must be built.

When identity is all that is left, hanging on to it can be a sensible response. At the very least—and against all odds—one survives. But as Silva discovered in her interviews with working-class adults, people can become so attached to their identity as survivors that they lack the capacity to criticize and challenge the conditions under which they are forced to struggle. Because these conditions, generally those of racialized patriarchal capitalism, are taken for granted, figured as either contingent or immutable, survival itself appears as the real political achievement.[28] Attachment to identity is nevertheless pathological. It's an attachment to a fantasy of wholeness or certainty, to the illusion of that pure site that can guarantee that we are right, that we are on the side of the angels. The fantasy blocks from view the way that identities are themselves split, contested, sites of class struggle. That someone identifies as a woman, as black, as transgender, or as a survivor tells us nothing about their politics.

That identities are sites of struggle rather than grounds of struggle is clear when we consider allyship. Despite its association with sovereign nations involved in wartime alliances, the term *ally* has become influential in US left activist circles. For at least five years, there has been intense discussion on social media and university campuses as well as among community organizers about what it means to be an ally and who can be an ally. Generally, allies are privileged people who want to do something about oppression. They may not consider themselves survivors or victims, but they want to help. So allies can be straight people who stand up for LGBTQ people, white people who support black and brown people, men who defend women, and so on. I have yet to see the term used for rich people involved in working-class struggle. Allies don't want to imagine themselves as homophobic, racist, or sexist. They see themselves as the good guys, part of the solution.

As is frequently emphasized in debates around allyship, claiming to be an ally does not make one an ally. Allyship is a process requiring time and effort. People have to work at it. It is not an identity. Much of the written and video work on allyship is thus didactic and instructional. It takes the form of a how-to guide or list of pointers—how to be an ally, the dos and don'ts of allyship, and so on. Like eliminate-the-clutter books or tips for clean eating, the instructions for being a good ally are mini lifestyle manuals, techniques for navigating the neoliberal environment of privilege and oppression. Individuals can learn what not to say and what not to do. They can feel engaged, changing their feelings if not the world without taking power, without any organized political struggle at all. The "politics" in these allyship how-tos consists of interpersonal interactions, individuated feelings, and mediated affects.

The pieces on how to be a good ally that circulate online (as blog posts, videos, editorials, and handouts for courses or campuses) address the viewer or reader as an individual with a privileged identity who wants to operate in solidarity with the marginalized and oppressed. As I detail below, this potential ally is positioned as wanting to know what they can do right now, on their own, and in their everyday lives to combat racism, sexism, homophobia, and other forms of oppression. The ally's field of operation is often imagined as social media (in knowing the right way to respond to racist or homophobic remarks on Twitter, for example); as charitable contribution (in donating to and setting up GoFundMe campaigns); as professional interaction (in hiring the marginalized and promoting the oppressed); as conversations at one's school or university (in knowing what not to say); and, sometimes, as street-level protests (in not dominating someone else's event). Even more often, the ally's own individual disposition, attitude, and behavior constitute the presumed operational field. The how-to guide instructs allies on how to feel, think, and act if they want to consider themselves as people who are on the side of the oppressed. Their awareness is what needs to change.

For example, as the open-source "Guide to Allyship," created in 2016 by Amelie Lamont, a self-identified cisgendered black woman who experienced the betrayal of a white ally who failed to support her in a confrontation with a racist, explains:

> To be an ally is to: Take on the struggle as your own. Stand up, even when you feel scared. Transfer the benefits of your privilege to those who lack it. Acknowledge that while you, too, feel pain, the conversation is not about you.[29]

Here allyship is a matter of the self, of what the self acknowledges, of the individual who stands alone, and of this single individual taking on a struggle that properly belongs to another. It's as if struggles were possessions—artifacts that individuals take on, over, and into themselves—all while being urged to see these acquisitions as something to which they, as the ally, have no right. At the same time, exactly what the struggle is, what the politics is, remains opaque, unstated, and a matter of the individual's feeling, attitude, or comfort level.

Here's another example from a BuzzFeed post titled "How to Be a Better Ally: An Open Letter to White Folks." The text is from a letter sent by a producer of the BuzzFeed video series, "Another Round," in reply to a question from a white person about being an ally.

> Have you ever had a conversation with a feminist man come grinding to a halt because he starts to complain about how feminists use language that excludes men, even the feminist men? ("Not all men . . .") I have! Being a good ally often means not being included in the conversation, because the conversation isn't about you. It's good to listen. If you feel uncomfortable and excluded because you're white, you should own those feelings.[30]

Again, allyship is a disposition, a confrontation not with state or capitalist power but with one's own discomfort. To be an ally is to work to cultivate in oneself habits of proper listening, to decenter oneself, to step aside and become aware of the lives and experiences of others.

Karolina Szczur's essay "Fundamentals of Effective Allyship," originally delivered as a talk at Tech Inclusion Melbourne, configures allyship in terms of the intensity of the ally's feelings and whether the ally is willing and able to undertake the necessary self-work:

> It's our responsibility to recognize, identify and act on the privilege we have. One of the ways of doing so is committing to an ongoing act of introspection, reflection and learning. You will find yourself challenged, uncomfortable, even defensive, but the more intense these feelings are, the more likely it is you're on the right track.[31]

Acting on privilege appears here as an interior act, an act of the self on the self. One's politics may be entirely in one's head. The ally is imaginary, not symbolic; an ideal ego or idealized version of who we want to be rather than an ego ideal or perspective from which we evaluate ourselves. In this respect, allyship reflects the shrinking or decline of the political. The space for politics has decreased yet the ally feels the need to act, desperately, intensely, and now. They act in and on what is available—social media, and themselves.

The process of becoming aware reiterates a key injunction of communicative capitalism: Educate yourself. Google it. Don't ask or burden the oppressed. The online magazine *Everyday Feminism* provides a list of ten things allies need to know. Number five on the list is: "Allies Educate Themselves Constantly." It explains:

> One of the most important types of education is listening . . . but there are endless resources (books, blogs, media outlets, speakers, YouTube videos, etc.) to help you learn. *What you*

should not do, though, is expect those with whom you want to ally yourself to teach you. That is not their responsibility. Sure, listen to them when they decide to drop some knowledge or perspective, but do not go to them and expect them to explain their oppression for you.[32]

The process of educating oneself is isolating, individuating. Learning is modeled as consuming information, not as discussion; coming to a common understanding; or studying the texts and documents of a political tradition. Educating oneself is disconnected from a collective critical practice, detached from political positions or goals. Criteria according to which one might evaluate books, blogs, speakers, and videos are absent. It's up to the individual ally to figure it out on their own. In effect, there is punishment without discipline. The would-be ally can be scolded and shamed, even as the scolder is relieved of any responsibility to provide concrete guidance and training (let's be clear, just telling someone to "Google it" is an empty gesture). Once we recall that "ally" is not a term of address—it doesn't replace "Mr.," "Ms.," "Dr.," or "Professor"; the term ally appears more to designate a limit, suggesting that you will never be one of us, than it does to enable solidarity. The relation between allies and those they are allies for, or to, is between those with separate interests, experiences, and practices.

The eighth item on the list of things allies need to know is: "Allies Focus on Those Who Share Their Identity." "Beyond listening, *arguably the most important thing that I can do to act in solidarity is to engage those who share my identity.*"[33] Identities appear clear and fixed, unambiguous and unchanging. Individuals are like little sovereign states, defending their territory, and only joining together under the most cautious and self-interested terms. Those taken to share an identity are presumed to share a politics, as if the identity were obvious and the politics didn't need to be built. Those willing to forward a politics other than one anchored in what can easily be ascribed to their identity are treated with suspicion, mistrusted for their presumed privilege, and criticized in advance for the array of wrongs that preserve that privilege. The very terms of allyship reinforce the mistrust that the how-to-be-better guides purport to address: it makes sense to mistrust people who view politics as immediate gratification, as an individualized quick fix to long histories of structural oppression. Because allies join together under self-interested terms, they can easily withdraw, drop out, let us down. We can't be sure of their commitment because it hinges on their individual feelings and comfort. Item eight in the article ("Allies Focus on Those Who Share Their Identity") tells us why allyship has such a hold in progressive circles: Mistrust of other identities becomes functional and gratifying in the name of a politics that maintains and polices identity, our own special and vulnerable thing, shoring up its weak and porous boundaries. "Ally" keeps attention away from the fearsome challenge of choosing a side, from accepting the discipline that comes from collective work, and from organizing for the abolition of racial patriarchal capitalism and the state designed to secure it.

So rather than bridging political identities or articulating a politics that moves beyond identity, allyship is a symptom of the displacement of politics into the individualist self-help techniques and social media moralism of communicative capitalism. The underlying vision is of self-oriented individuals, politics as possession, transformation reduced to attitudinal change, and a fixed, naturalized sphere of privilege and oppression. Anchored in a view of identity as the primary vector of politics, the emphasis on allies displaces attention away from strategic organizational and tactical questions and onto prior attitudinal litmus tests, from the start precluding the collectivity necessary for revolutionary left politics. Of course, those on the left need allies. Sometimes it is necessary to forge temporary alliances in order to advance. A struggle with communism as its horizon will involve an array of tactical alliances among different classes, sectors, and tendencies. But provisional allies focused on their own interests are not the same as comrades—although they might become comrades. My critique of the ally as the symptom and limit of contemporary identity politics should thus not be taken as a rejection of practices of alliance in the course of political struggle. That would be absurd. I am rejecting allyship as the form and model for struggles against oppression, immiseration, dispossession, and exploitation.

Communicative capitalism enjoins uniqueness. We are commanded to be ourselves, express ourselves, do it ourselves. Conforming, copying, and letting another speak for us are widely thought to be somehow bad, indicative of weakness, ignorance, or unfreedom. The impossibility of an individual politics, the fact that political change is always and only collective, is suppressed, displaced into the inchoate conviction that we are determined by systems and forces completely outside our capacity to affect them. Climate changes. Not us.

If we recognize that the attachment to individual identity is the form of our political incapacity, we can acquire new capacities for action, the collective capacities of those on the same side of a struggle. We can become more than allies who are concerned with defending our own individual identity and lecturing others on what they must do to aid us in this defense. We can become comrades struggling together to change the world. I thus agree with Mark Fisher's crucial reminder: "We need to learn, or re-learn, how to build comradeship and solidarity instead of doing capital's work for it by condemning and abusing each other."[34]

Where the ally is hierarchical, specific, and acquiescent, the comrade is egalitarian, generic, and utopian. The egalitarian and generic dimensions of comrade are what make it utopian, what enable the relation between comrades to cut through the determinations of the everyday (which is another way of saying capitalist social relations). In the following chapter, I take up potential objections to this idea of a generic comrade. My examples there and throughout the book draw largely, but not exclusively, from the Communist Party of the United States. Given that there have been communist parties and organizations in virtually every country in the world, the examples could have come from almost anywhere. Most parties have encountered similar problems at one time or another. I use examples from the United States because they demonstrate how even this intensely individualist, capitalist, racist, Cold War political culture produced a mode of political belonging that can serve as an alternative to allyship. My aim is to surface another possible history, one made by comrades in settings internally divided and seemingly far from revolution, settings not unlike our own.

CHAPTER TWO

The Generic Comrade

GIVEN THE PRESENT INTENSITY of politicized identities, particularly in the Global North, some might worry that the figure of the comrade excludes sex and race, and that it incorporates a masculine, white imaginary. This chapter responds to these concerns by arguing for the power of comrade under conditions of patriarchal racial capitalism. My method is speculative-compositive. I don't provide a linear history or a detailed critique of the various real existing socialisms. Instead, I extract examples from their contexts, salvaging them for present struggles for another future. Rather than remaining stuck in the ruins of communism, we can scavenge the ruins for past hopes and old lessons and put these remnants to use as we organize and build.

Comrade Woman

I begin with the masculine objection. Although it comes up frequently in my public talks, the worry that the comrade is a man is a strange one. I immediately think: Rosa Luxemburg, Angela Davis, Alexandra Kollontai, Claudia Jones, Clara Zetkin, Sylvia Pankhurst, Dolores Ibárruri, Zhang Qinqiu, Marta Harnecker,

Grace Lee Boggs, Leila Khaled, Luciana Castellina, Tamara Bunke. At least some of these names should be familiar. They are women, and they are comrades. In her classic book *Women, Race and Class*, Angela Davis lists some of the women activists involved in CPUSA in its early years: "'Mother' Ella Reeve Bloor, Anita Whitney, Margaret Prevey, Kate Sadler Greenhalgh, Rose Pastor Stokes and Jeanette Pearl."[1]

If the figure of the comrade is not primarily or constitutively male—but rather generic, a form for political relations between those on the same side that abstracts from socially given or naturalized identities as it posits a common field of equality and belonging—then the case for it is probably not best made with the use of proper names. The proper name loses the element of relationality crucial to comrade. A better response to the concern that comrade is masculine, to the worry that comrade does not in fact abstract from socially given identities, might then invoke the masses of women all over the world who have been part of armed communist struggle—and of course those who continue to be, as in the Philippines and in India, as Arundhati Roy describes in her book *Walking with the Comrades*. Or maybe the case against a masculinist reduction of comrade becomes compelling when we recall the vast array of groups and events for mobilizing women indispensable to the world communist milieu in the twentieth century, the innumerable commissions, committees, conferences, and publications aiming to organize women. For example, the First International Conference of Socialist Women took place in 1907. Alexandra Kollontai reports that the primary topic in this lively, energetic conference was voting rights for women workers, which she advocated. In contrast, the delegation of German women comrades proposed that the demand "Without distinction of sex" become part of the general social democratic approach to universal suffrage, a right for which working-class men in Europe were still fighting. The demand was controversial. Kollontai observes that "awareness of the importance of full and equal political rights for women workers in the name of the interests of the whole class has not yet had time to take firm root."[2] Consequently, opportunistic compromises could occasion the abandonment of working-class women's suffrage in the interest of universal male suffrage (to the detriment of class unity and the broader electoral power of the working class) or, as was occurring in the English women's suffrage movement, the broad defense of women's interests could lose sight of class struggle. Socialists, Kollontai argued, needed to work for suffrage for women workers, confident that securing women's right to vote would help working men and all women.

In a conversation with Clara Zetkin, Lenin insisted that women are comrades even as he rejected the idea that the Communist Party should itself have a separate women's organization. His position on women is consistent with his approach to the organization of people of different nationalities living in Russia. The Russian Social Democratic Labor Party was founded as a party for the *entire* proletariat. In 1913, Lenin reasoned that conditions in Russia demand

> that Social-Democracy should unite unconditionally workers of all nationalities in all proletarian organizations without exception (political, trade union, co-operative, educational, etc., etc.). The Party should not be federative in structure and should not form national Social-Democratic groups but should unite the proletarians of all nations in the given locality, conduct propaganda and agitation in all the languages of the local proletariat, promote the common struggle of the workers of all nations against every kind of national privilege and should recognize the autonomy of local and regional Party organizations.[3]

Lenin applied the same principle to the woman question, saying, "A woman communist is a member of the Party just as a man

communist, with equal rights and duties. There can be no difference of opinion on that score."[4] At the same time, he emphasized
the necessity of commissions, of "special modes of agitation and
forms of organization" charged with arousing women workers,
peasants, and petite bourgeoisie and bringing them into contact
with the party. And he accentuated the necessity of the party
putting forth demands that respond to the condition of women.
Through such demands, the party demonstrates that it recognizes
the humiliation women endure, that it understands and abhors
men's privilege. The party shows that "we hate, yes hate everything,
and will abolish everything, which tortures and oppresses the
woman worker, the housewife, the peasant woman, the wife of the
petty trader, yes, and in many cases the women of the possessing
classes."[5]

That comrades are women and women are comrades also
becomes clear when we recall the variations in views on gender
and the family that the term has contained. On the one hand, we
can note early Soviet experiments in dismantling bourgeois familial and sexual norms and creating new egalitarian relations
characterized by comradeship and solidarity. Here, comradeship
entails abolishing practices that subordinate women by socializing
the tasks of social reproduction. On the other hand, we can point
to the years of the US Popular Front, where the nuclear family and
women's nurturing and maternal roles were emphasized, especially
women's capacity to raise a new generation of class-conscious
communists.[6] Like the Communist Party of the Soviet Union,
CPUSA took a conservative turn in the late thirties, moving away
from its critique of the bourgeois family and reputation for
advocacy of free love.[7] Nevertheless, the maternal emphasis of
CPUSA at this time did not prevent Communist women from
using the party to hold their husbands to account for male
chauvinism. Barbara Foley reports that at least "one male
Communist was removed from leadership for refusing to help
with child care."[8] Even if their strengths and roles were

differentiated, in the party men and women were comrades and should be able to expect equality. Incidentally, US Cold War popular culture also recognizes that the comrade isn't necessarily masculine. Movies, television shows, pulp novels, magazines, and ads feature stereotypes that simultaneously mock the androgyny of women comrades and forward the fantasy of sexy KGB spies using their feminine wiles to seduce Americans into betraying their government.

In his account of the US revolutionary left in the 1930s, Murray Kempton holds up the comrade woman, writing,

> The thirties appear in recollection to have swarmed with the Comrade Woman. She seemed constructed of whalebone, and often stronger than the male. Few of us who were not as strong as we should have been in those days can forget a moment's confrontation by some avenging female agent from the movement calling us back to our duties like a maiden elder sister calling us to dinner.[9]

As is clear from Kempton's rhetoric, that women were comrades did not mean that communist men were vigilant in combatting sexist stereotypes. Nevertheless, the party committed itself to fighting for women's equality and, in so doing, created a space for radical women activists. Over the course of the 1930s, the amount of women in CPUSA increased to 40 percent.[10] They would achieve parity in 1944.[11] Black women in and around the party such as Claudia Jones, Esther Cooper Jackson, Louise Thompson Patterson, Thyra Edwards, Marvel Cooke, and Ella Baker worked actively to connect antifascist and antiracist struggles as well as to direct the party's attention to the specific forms of oppression experienced by black women. In an article published in 1936 in *Women Today*, a Communist Party magazine, Louise Thompson Patterson theorizes black women's triple exploitation—"as workers, as women, and as Negroes."[12] Claudia Jones would develop this theory further in late 1940s. As Erik S. McDuffie argues, Jones's essay "An End to the Neglect of the Problems of the Negro Woman!," published before her arrest and deportation under the Smith Act, "profoundly influenced the CPUSA's thinking on race, gender, and class," leading to an array of articles on the triple exploitation of black women in party periodicals.[13]

Following Engels's analysis in *The Origin of the Family, Private Property, and the State*, CPUSA promoted the view that women's subordination to men was neither natural nor universal but instead an effect of exploitation. Margaret Cowl's 1935 pamphlet *Women and Equality*, part of a series on women published by the party in the thirties, draws out the connections between private property and women's subordination.[14] Once men privatized property, women lost their freedom, coming under the control of men via the institution of marriage. Although unequal to and dependent on the men in their class, bourgeois women benefited from exploitation insofar as they employed servants. Working-class women depended on the wage, even as industrial development replaced domestic production, diminishing the value of their handicraft work, and factory speedups amplified their exploit-ation. Working women, which Cowl estimated to have comprised approximately 46 percent of married women (and up to 70 percent of married women in the South) faced a set of particular chal-lenges: propaganda aiming to push women out of industry (which made it hard for them to unionize for fear of being fired); employ-ers' manipulation of women's "tender feelings for their loved ones" in order to keep wages low; the legal inscription of lower wages for white women and still lower wages for black women; the absence of maternity insurance, which would have allowed women to safe-guard their jobs following pregnancy; "vicious anti-birth-control laws" that subjected women to "bootleg-racketeer prices for birth-control information"; and the drudgery of housework.[15] To address these challenges, the Communist Party supported equal pay for equal work, maternity insurance, "abolition of the anti-birth-control laws," free childcare for working mothers, "free birth-control clinics," and the abolition of laws discriminating against women.[16] It was also necessary, Cowl concludes, for white women to fight for the same rights for Negro women and to support Negro liberation.

Kate Weigand's *Red Feminism: American Communism and the Making of Women's Liberation* unravels some of the misconceptions about CPUSA that came to be widely held by feminists in the United States during the 1980s and that are repeated today.[17] She documents the controversy around Mary Inman, a party member whose 1940 book, *In Women's Defense*, was critiqued in a party publication in 1941 and who subsequently made forcing a change in the party's analysis of women's conditions into her life's work. Weigand points out that while much of Inman's book reflected the party's position in the 1930s, the book also developed new ideas that the party would adopt later in the decade—in particular, the impact of cultural norms and practices, the role of the family in transmitting gender norms, and the subjugation effected by the preoccupation with beauty.[18]

In Women's Defense also advanced a new theory of housework as socially productive labor. Housewives produce "the labor power of present and future generations of workers."[19] They do this work "for capitalists who paid them through their husbands' wages."[20] Inman's book received a positive review in the *Daily Worker*. The Communist Party's schools used it in courses. Inman was invited to teach at a workers' school in Los Angeles. Party members started debating her arguments. Conflict erupted when leaders of the California party, Eva Shafran and Al Bryan, "came to Inman's classroom and explained to her students that, despite what their teacher told them, housework is not productive labor."[21] Inman's course was cancelled and she began making appeals up the party hierarchy. Her meeting with national leaders, which included Elizabeth Gurley Flynn and Ella Reeve (Mother) Bloor, did not go well. Not only did the national leadership reject Inman's view of housework (for tactical and theoretical reasons) but they found her to be intransigent, employing personal attacks on anyone who didn't share her view, and messianic in her conception of her role.[22]

Nevertheless, the party recognized Inman as a comrade. Weigand quotes a letter from Bloor asking a friend to "show Mary Inman that we are sincere honest comrades and really tried to get at the 'common denominator' of the proposals and not to have her go home bitter and resentful."[23] Flynn also reached out to party comrades for help with persuading Inman to put the controversy aside and find a way to be "useful and happy in our Party."[24] But Inman wanted nothing less than full party acceptance of her view. She didn't receive it. Instead, the party's theoretical journal, *The Communist*, published a critique of the idea that housework is productive labor, even though it didn't mention Inman by name. The author Avram Landy observes that of course housework is useful labor, but Marxism-Leninism is not a theory of the usefulness of labor for the capitalist system; it's a theory of the exploitation of labor.[25] From this angle, housework needs to be understood as drudgery, as part of a condition women face that must and can be changed. Landy further asserts that a housewife's right to make demands "does not stem from her 'usefulness' but from her character as a human being, a member of the working class and toiling population who is oppressed and subjugated. It is this oppressed and subjugated status that is the sole source of her 'right' to make demands."[26] Inman resigned from the party.

Inman spent the next forty years continuing to fight this battle. She produced a newsletter, articles, books, pamphlets, and letters to party leaders and left publications attacking the Communist Party for its position on the woman question. She came up with a conspiracy theory that the party was intent on liquidating all work on women's issues and that this stretched back to J. Edgar Hoover's influence on Nikolai Bukharin. She didn't get involved in the new wave of feminist activism but instead preoccupied herself with 1940s and '50s "Browder revisionism," a symptomatic preoccupation given that Earl Browder, a former leader of the Communist Party, had been expelled from the party in 1945.[27] As Weigand details, in the 1970s, Inman began sending her writings to various feminist scholars. Bruised by their own experiences on the New Left, they repeated Inman's story of being forced out of the party by men who refused to debate her and concluded that "the Party opposed any discussion of or organization around the problems of women's oppression before World War II, and in the late 1940s and 1950s as well."[28] As late as 2015, the editors of *Viewpoint Magazine* repeated Inman's version of the Communist Party's position on women, claiming that Inman exposed "the complicity between economic reductionism and identitarian reformism in the CPUSA" and that the Communist Party effaced "the economic role of women's work" and naturalized "the social phenomenon of mother," thereby reducing the "'struggle against capitalist oppression of women' [to the ideological contestation of] 'masculine superiority.'"[29] Weigand's careful research, not to mention the party's own publications and organizing, undermines this claim. Even Landy's initial critique of Inman's position on housework shows the party's view to be more nuanced than *Viewpoint Magazine*'s channeling of Inman allows. Not only does Landy set out the subjugation of women by "capitalist productive relations" but he also draws out demands and issues arising out of housewives' concrete conditions: "better housing, cheaper rents, the high cost of living, day nurseries, free lunches for children."[30]

Empirically speaking, then, the worry that comrade is male seems to stem either from a lack of knowledge or from a forgetting of history. Forgetting history could occasion the presumption that comrade operates like citizen, which was associated with men's rights and responsibilities as property owners, holders of public office, and members of the military. Forgetting history could also be thought to imply that *comrade* is a synonym for *proletarian*, which has itself suffered from an excessive and exclusive masculinization. But, already in the nineteenth century, comrade was used by female and male socialists with commitments to widespread social transformation. The genericity of comrade lets it encompass not just women and men but various and changing assumptions regarding gender.

Perhaps, though, the forgetting of comrade women is symptomatic. Perhaps it grows out of a fear of losing what is most precious and unique. Differently put, the critical gesture toward comrade's suspected masculinity may not be about masculinity at all. It may actually express a fear about the loss of individual specificity. We have to confront this fear: Comrade insists on the equalizing sameness that comes from fighting on the same side of a political struggle. It ruptures the everyday world with the challenge of egalitarian modes of acting and belonging. It liberates comrades from the constraining expectations of the identities inscribed on and demanded of us by patriarchal racial capitalism. You will encounter hatred and bigotry in everyday life, but with your comrades you should be able to expect something more, something better. Kathi Weeks observes that Fredric Jameson captures the "fear of becoming different" associated with the fear of utopia as:

> a thoroughgoing anxiety in the face of everything we stand to lose in the course of so momentous a transformation that— even in the imagination—it can be thought to leave little intact of current passions, habits, practices, and values.[31]

The fear that comrade is masculine reflects the fear of a political relation that does not prioritize difference and individuality, that does not begin from a concern with the individual but that is focused on common work toward a common goal.

That women and men address each other as comrade does not mean that gender-based hierarchy vanishes. Robin D. G. Kelley points out that in the 1930s, white women comrades were generally "relegated to mimeograph machines and the occasional public speaking."[32] Black women rose to midlevel leadership positions, many drawn into the party because of its campaign to free the Scottsboro Boys (nine young black men falsely convicted of raping two white women in Alabama and sentenced with execution).[33] Comrade doesn't abolish the antagonism of sex. It enables another possibility to intrude. It holds out the promise of another form of relation between sexed beings, a political relation between comrades. This new form provides a standard according to which the old ways of being are judged. Comrade does not eliminate difference. It provides a container indifferent to its contents. Other elements of our relation—friendship, kinship, citizenship, neighbor, as I detail in the following chapter—are not extinguished. They may inform or enliven our comradeship—sometimes party members marry or become lovers. As Angela Davis writes of the loss of George Jackson: "For me, George's death has meant the loss of a comrade and revolutionary leader, but also the loss of an irretrievable love."[34] We may be lovers looking into each other's eyes, but as comrades we look together toward a common horizon (to use Slavoj Žižek's frequent example). Likewise, comrade does not eliminate conflict. It names an aspiration not always fulfilled but one that comrades can be expected to recognize, to strive for. Comrade is not an empirical designator of what happens. It is a figure in the world for something better: We don't have to appeal to familial or sexed relations as a norm for interaction. We can appeal to solidarity and comradeship.

The worry about the masculinity of the figure of the comrade might also express a concern about sex. Men cannot be comrades with women because sex gets in the way. Men's individual sexual desire disrupts comradeship. Lenin addresses this problem in his conversation with Zetkin (in a voluble, excessive aside). He talks about a young comrade who "reels and staggers from one love affair to the next," commenting:

> That won't do for the political struggle, for the revolution . . . the revolution demands concentration, increase of force. From

the masses, from individuals . . . no weakening, no waste, no destruction of forces. Self-control, self-discipline, is not slavery, not even in love.[35]

There can be a political relation between sexed beings (a relation even when a sexual relation is impossible—that is, even insofar as "there is no such thing as a sexual relationship," as Lacan teaches). Sexed beings can be comrades, on the same side of a political struggle. Comrade is not the two of love; anyone, but not everyone, can be a comrade, as I argue in chapter three.

That anyone but not everyone can be a comrade imbues comrade with what Lacan designates as a feminine structure—comrade is non-all.[36] Comrade does not hold out the One as an exception (again, anyone but not everyone). In this vein, Lenin says to Zetkin, following his excursus on increasing rather than destroying forces such as joy of life and power of life: "Forgive me, Clara, I have wandered far from the starting point of our conversation. Why didn't you call me to order? My tongue has run away with me."[37] Lenin's enjoyment here is the feminine *jouissance* of language. He calls on comradely assistance from Zetkin in bringing his excess back to order. Lenin makes this point himself:

> You know, Clara, I shall make use of the fact that I was with a woman. I'll explain my lateness by reference to the well-known feminine volubility. Although this time it was the man, and not the woman, who spoke such a lot.[38]

To sum up: Comrade is not masculine. Comrade is a generic figure operating as an ego ideal. It provides the perspective comrades take when they see themselves acting politically, a perspective generated by their relation to others on the same side of a political struggle. This equality is the utopian element of comradeship. The determinations of a sexist, racist, capitalist society unavoidably intrude, but comrade names a relation no longer determined by these factors, providing a site from which they can be judged and addressed.

The Black Comrade

What about race? Is comrade irredeemably constrained by white, European political histories? The same style of argument I used to confront the masculinist concern is useful here. The worry that comrade is white proceeds as if people of color, black people in particular, have never been comrades in the socialist and communist sense. The view that communism is white or European omits histories and presents of struggle—in India, China, Algeria, Cuba, Guinea-Bissau, Palestine, Angola, Vietnam, Korea, Indonesia, South Africa, Nepal, Colombia, Afghanistan, the Philippines, Iran, the United States, Yemen, virtually everywhere. Over the past several decades, a large body of crucial work has documented the inextricable ties between communist, black liberation, and anticolonial struggles, demonstrating the mutual constitution of a politics that has unraveled in the wake of the defeats of labor and the Soviet Union. With specific regard to black communism in the United States, there have been indispensable contributions by Carole Boyce Davies, Barbara Foley, Dayo F. Gore, Gerald Horne, Walter T. Howard, Yasuhiro Katagiri, Robin D. G. Kelley, Minkah Makalani, Erik S. McDuffie, Mark Naison, Mark Solomon, and Mary Helen Washington, to mention but a few. In addition to this scholarly archive, there are the invaluable memoirs from black Communists Angela Davis, Harry Haywood, and Hosea Hudson (again, a partial list). Paul M. Heideman recently published a large collection of primary texts on the race question written in the US socialist tradition, titled *Class Struggle and the Color Line*. This supplements Philip S. Foner's two volumes of documentary history, *American Communism and Black Americans*. Racism and anticommunism continue to work to expel this body of knowledge, to keep it from registering in all its truth and complexity. Each operates with caricatures of race and communism, as if they were unities rather than heterogeneous multiplicities. Black comrades are discovered then forgotten, carried more in the disciplinary pockets of the academy than in the living body of a party.

In the US context, the concern that comrade is white can be broken down into two suspicions: The first assumes that black people are not or cannot be comrades with each other; the second that black people are not or cannot be comrades with white people. The first suspicion implies that the politics of those ascribed to the same racial category is determined by the shared characteristics of the category. The supposition of racial kinship—brothers and sisters—occupies the entire political imaginary, as if there were no political divisions between those who belong to the same racial category. Clearly this is wrong. There have been and continue to be political differences among black people, just as there are between people of any identity based on ethnicity, sexuality, or gender. Questions of separatism and assimilation, of acceptance or rejection of capitalism, and of strategies and tactics of liberation barely scratch the surface of the politics dividing people ascribed the same racial identity.

Another way to read the concern that black people are not each other's comrades is as a statement regarding the black radical tradition. There is a black radical tradition independent of and irreducible to Marxism that must be understood on its own terms.[39] Indeed, Biko Agozino makes a powerful argument for the influence of this tradition on Marx.[40] The fact of the black radical tradition, however, does not conflict with my argument that comrade is not racially exclusive. It supports it, inciting us to recognize how and why some black radicals turned to communism and their impact on communist movement. The militant black woman organizer Lucy Parsons, for example, prioritized class struggle. Parsons thought sex and race "were facts of existence manipulated by employers who sought to justify their greater exploitation of women and people of color."[41] She went so far as to claim that not even lynching was primarily a race crime. Black men were lynched not because they were black but because they were poor.[42]

Cyril Briggs is another great example. One of a number of West Indian immigrants influential in the Harlem Renaissance, Briggs founded the magazine the *Crusader* in September 1918.[43] The magazine was dedicated to "race patriotism," specifically "Africa for the Africans." Shortly after its start, the *Crusader* began featuring articles linking capitalism and colonialism and promoting a proletarian identity shared by black and white workers.[44] Given Briggs's race-first commitments, this was a radical innovation. Briggs was merging revolutionary socialism and black nationalism. For example, in his editorial "Make Their Cause Your Own," published in July 1919, Briggs observes:

> With no race are the interests of Labor so clearly identified with racial interests as in the case of the Negro race. No race would be more greatly benefited by the triumph of Labor and the destruction of parasitic Capital Civilization with its Imperialism incubus that is squeezing the life-blood out of millions of our race in Africa and the islands of the sea, than the Negro race.[45]

During the violent Red Summer of 1919, Briggs was presenting labor as a race issue. He saw the connections between working-class struggle and the struggle "of the Negro race." The end of capitalism would benefit black people.

In the summer of 1919, massive strikes erupted across the United States—a general strike in Seattle as well as steel and coal strikes involving hundreds of thousands of workers. Anarchist bombing campaigns intensified the situation. Black soldiers newly returned from the front received not a hero's welcome but discrimination, oppression, and violence. They were passed over for good jobs, pushed into menial work. Rioting white people attacked black people. Black people fought back. Lynchings increased across the South. White southerners even burned people at the stake, the state of Mississippi authorizing burning a black man alive. The governor claimed that he was powerless to stop it but had been assured that "necessary arrangements" had been made and that the mob would act in conformity to these arrangements. Three thousand people came to watch.[46] The black press—which included over two hundred newspapers—urged black people to protect themselves, to oppose lynch law with "cold steel and fire," with "iron will and inflexible determination."[47] The headlines of white newspapers screamed, "Reds Try to Stir Negroes to Revolt." Blaming the Bolsheviks for the chaos in the United States, the mainstream media told its readers that black publications were financed by Russia with the goal of establishing Bolshevik rule in the United States.[48] Linking the black struggle for liberation to Bolshevism, the white press made black people who fought back look like traitors. The US Department of Justice started to treat black people "as potential enemies of the state."[49] White southerners inverted the problem: it wasn't that Negroes were going to usher in communist domination; communism would lead to Negro domination.[50]

This was the context, then, within which Briggs boldly claimed the Soviets as allies in the black liberation struggle and anti-Bolshevism as a vehicle for racism and attacks on black radicalism. He was not content to echo the black press and emphasize only the racial dimension of the violence inflicted on African Americans. He saw the violence as connected to the oppressive, exploitative nature of the capitalist system. By the end of the year, Briggs was associating anticommunism with white supremacy. He wrote:

> That Negro editors and cartoonists should fall for the lies
> about Soviet Russia put out by the white capitalist press is all

the more surprising when it is considered that these same Negro cartoonists and editors are members of a race even more viciously lied about by the same white capitalist press.[51]

Anticommunism, the ideology of black workers' white capitalist enemy, was contrary to black interests.

At the same time he was publishing the *Crusader*, Briggs organized the African Blood Brotherhood (ABB). Through both, he produced an original synthesis of African identity and Leninist internationalism.[52] The synthesis relied in part on Briggs's vision of an originary African communism destroyed by slavery and colonialism. Communism, in this vision, is authentically African—not European. Anchored in the past, Briggs's synthesis was nevertheless oriented to the future: the only path for black liberation is through an independent socialist Negro state within a larger universalist socialist commonwealth. Black liberation depends on socialism—the interests of all people of African descent lead to socialism. African freedom is impossible in a capitalist system. Only an anti-imperialist alliance with the working class, where black workers lead advanced white workers, will secure the dream of black national independence. The ABB presented the black freedom struggle as aiming at socialist transformation—not "assimilation into the bourgeois order"—and it presented black workers as the leaders of a multiracial working class, not followers of a black elite.[53] Against critics who saw the comrade as white because they merged trade unionism, workerism, socialism, and communism, Briggs presented a more complex picture: The comrade is a fighter for black liberation, committed to "Negro consciousness" and a race-first politics, who turns to Lenin and the Soviet experiment as resources for the black struggle for liberation.

For black activists in Marxist-Leninist political formations, comrade has been a term of address that sometimes accompanies the familial language of black nationalism and the black church and sometimes replaces it. In *Incognegro*, Frank Wilderson describes the devastating impact of the murder of Chris Hani, the chief of staff of uMkhonto weSizwe (MK) and leader of the South African Communist Party, on his MK branch, especially its effect on Jabu Mosando, who had never rested easily with the shift away from Steve Biko's Black Consciousness Movement to the Freedom Charter's "wretched nonracialism."[54] Shortly after Hani's murder, there was a meeting that included the black comrades Jabu and Stimela and a white comrade, Trevor. Wilderson writes:

> Stimela finished the briefing and asked Jabu if what he had said was clear. Yeah, Jabu said. Stimela went to the door and checked the hallway. He motioned to Jabu. "Good luck, comrade." "Brother," Jabu corrected him. "Jabu, I know how you feel." "Do you?" "I feel the same way." "What way is that?" "Go, Jabu, quickly."[55]

The anguish of this account links to the suspicion that black people cannot be comrades with white people: Comradeship is a ruse, a trick, a dirty game that subordinates black interests to white interests.[56] Wilderson provides an example that belies this conclusion. He describes a visit to the Soviet Union in the 1970s in which a Russian man he was walking with reached out to hold his hand:

> I had had an urge to say I'm a linebacker not a homosexual; then I looked into the man's eyes and realized that this was not a come on. It was simply a profound gesture of camaraderie. And I had wanted to weep. For at that moment, as that man, who was willing to weave his few words of English into my few words of Russian, and I ascended the stairs to the cinema, I thought of the wretched children at Kenwood Grammar School who, eleven years before, had chosen to hold up recess until hell froze over rather than form a line where one of them would have to hold my hand. If communism will cleanse my

hands, I had thought, then I am a communist.[57]
For a moment, comradeship provided an escape from racism. Comrades were briefly liberated from the damaging world of hatred and bigotry.

Wilderson's story echoes one told by the black communist labor organizer Ernest Rice McKinney to dramatize the influence of the Communist Party among African Americans during the Depression. McKinney describes leaving an American Workers Party meeting in Pittsburgh:

> We were walking down the street, black and white together, and there were some black men walking with white women. We were in a tough working class district and as we passed a group of white youth, they said to us, "Hello Comrades." Their tone was sarcastic, but not hostile. They assumed we were Communists, because the Communists had made such an impression by practicing social equality.[58]

US Communists weren't always successful in practicing social equality. In 1949, Claudia Jones, a party leader, called out white men and women and black men comrades for their failure "to extend courtesy to Negro women and to integrate Negro women into organizational leadership."[59] Communists especially should be expected to recognize that "the question of social relations with Negro men and women is above all a question of adhering to social equality."[60] To be a comrade was to practice social equality in everyday life as well as in party work. The expectation of comrades, held even by those who were not comrades themselves and which was not always fulfilled, was radical egalitarianism. Comrades were those not only courageous enough to practice a mode of belonging deeply at odds with the prevailing culture but dedicated enough to recognize how personal relations help produce political power. Black women's leadership had to be understood as indispensable to revolutionary struggle.

On their own, these stories aren't enough to alleviate concerns with socialist and communist subordination of black interests to white interests. Closer attention to discussions within the Communist milieu may be of some assistance here. Again, I draw from experiences in CPUSA in the '20s and '30s with Briggs as an indispensable guide. In 1921, Briggs joined the Workers Party, one of the two parties that would merge to become the Communist Party, while continuing to work through the ABB and publish the *Crusader*. The Workers Party committed itself to destroying race prejudice and binding black and white workers into a union of revolutionary forces.[61] The party's platform incorporated Briggs's insights into "the role of slavery and lynch terror in the nation's accumulation of capital" and "the use of racial prejudice to subject blacks to extreme exploitation and to divide the working class."[62] At the same time, Briggs took up the question of "white friendship" in the *Crusader*. He observed that black people had been "grievously deceived" by past white declarations of friendship that ended up being for "personal gain or the curbing of Negro 'radicalism.'"[63] There were good reasons for black workers to be skeptical. Nevertheless, Briggs argues that black workers should recognize how white workers actually need black help to attain their goals. He describes this need as being politically useful to black people: "There are schisms in the white race which, by encouraging, we can ultimately benefit ourselves."[64] Black workers should not let the fact and fear of white opportunism hinder an analysis that could advance the black cause.

There's more. Briggs thought that black and white workers could be comrades. He points out:

Already white men have fought together with Negroes in defense of their common interests, and have staunchly refused to accept divisions in their ranks and betray their Negro comrades, although white employers have offered to concede to the workers' demands in the case of white workers if the latter would betray their Negro comrades.[65]

Briggs thus proposes an "acid test": Is a white person "willing to see the Negro defend himself with arms against aggression, and willing even to see Negroes killing his own (white) people in defense of Negro rights?"[66]

US Communists in the early 1930s took this test seriously. Mark Solomon gives the example of instructions given by a party organizer in 1932. Visiting a party section, the organizer

> told the group that Negroes had been betrayed perennially by whites seeking their support: "what every Communist must do is to be willing to die in defense of any Negro's rights, and it doesn't have to be anything flamboyant or very important— any insult, and there are plenty, directed by a white person against a Negro, is reason enough for a Communist to react, to slap his or her face, hit hard and if you be killed, that's alright too, because . . . without the Negro people we are only treading water as far as making the revolution in the U.S."[67]

The Communist Party embraced the view that black-white comradeship depended on white people's willingness to die for their black comrades. If they wanted to build class unity, white Communists had to prove to black people that they would defend the commitment to black liberation—"Negro rights" in the language of the 1930s party organizer—to the death. Anything less would put them on the side of racism, lynching, and Jim Crow exclusion from decently waged jobs. In effect, white Communists would have to give up their property in whiteness, abolish their own racial ignorance and privilege, if they wanted to create the conditions of possibility for unifying the working class. The advance of the white working class cannot come at the expense of black life. The failure to defend black liberation would defeat all workers.

Historians of black radicalism in the United States have exposed the lie behind claims that the Communist Party only engaged in black liberation struggles for its own ends. Robin D. G. Kelley, Mark Naison, Mark Solomon, and others present a view of African Americans and communism that rejects the scene of "manipulation, disillusionment, and betrayal" animating the writing of Richard Wright, Ralph Ellison, and Harold Cruse.[68] For a time, the Communist Party was the leading interracial organization in the fight against white supremacy in the United States.

Any concern regarding white subordination and betrayal of black interests would be incomplete absent the acknowledgement of a second concern: that the black bourgeoisie—middle-class black elites—advance their specific class interest by delivering a pacified, cooperative black lower class over to white law. This concern about the co-optation of black working-class radicalism of course isn't about comradeship. It's framed around respectability and the advancement of the race via assimilation into white society. It's a concern about accepting middle-class values and working within the system. Lovett Fort-Whiteman, one of CPUSA's early African-American members, supplied a cogent analysis of the political situation facing black people in the mid-1920s: Black advocates of a radical political direction were opposed by "Negro leaders" because the majority of these leaders depend "on the bounty of the white capitalist class," on white philanthropy, on donations to their colleges and institutions. These racial sell-outs "dare not support labor unionism among Negroes, they dare not advocate other than a capitalist ticket in politics."[69]

The Black Belt Thesis

The practical organizational life of CPUSA from the late 1920s through the mid-1930s was fraught and conflictual. Responding to criticisms from African-American Communists that their white comrades were insufficiently engaged in organizational work within the black community, the Comintern pushed the party to eliminate white chauvinism from its ranks and elevate the "Negro question" to the center of its organizing. At the time, there were real dangers to interracial organizing in the Jim Crow South. These conditions—class struggle under white supremacy—illuminate the power and promise of the comrade as a figure for a political relation liberated from the determinations of specificity. The scandalous Black Belt thesis illustrates this point.

After several years of debate, the Comintern, and thus the Communist Party, took the position that black people in the Black Belt of the United States (a large swathe of majority-black counties in the South, called the "Black Belt" because of the rich, dark soil) constituted an oppressed nation with the right to self-determination. I call this thesis scandalous because it is often denigrated as being out of touch with reality, dogmatic, ludicrous, impossible, and so forth—even as it echoed the nationalist themes of Marcus Garvey's United Negro Improvement Association and was picked up more than thirty years later by African American revolutionaries.[70] The Black Belt thesis also appears scandalous when held up against workerist assumptions that communists privilege the class struggle above all other struggles. Opposing the thesis in 1939, C. L. R. James argued:

> For us to propose that the Negro have this black state for himself is asking too much from the white workers, especially when the Negro himself is not making the same demand. The slogans of "abolition of debts," "confiscation of large properties," etc., are quite sufficient to lead them both to fight together and on the basis of economic struggle to make a united fight for the abolition of social discrimination.[71]

James was not in the Communist Party. His statement was prepared for a meeting he had with Trotsky. Even in the party, though, there was initial opposition to the idea that black people constituted an oppressed nation from those who insisted that the issue was racial, not national.

In his memoir, *Black Bolshevik*, Harry Haywood, the primary force behind the Black Belt thesis, sets out the stakes of the debate. The first issue is how to think about African Americans. Are they an oppressed racial minority or an oppressed national minority? The national minority position employed a theory of the nation developed by Stalin. Haywood presents Stalin's definition of a nation as

> a historically constituted stable community of people, based on four main characteristics: a common territory, a common economic life, a common language, and a common psychological makeup (national character) manifested in common features in a national culture. Since the development of imperialism, the liberation of the oppressed nations had become a question whose final resolution would only come through proletarian resolution.[72]

Already in 1920, Lenin had proposed to the Comintern a resolution stating that black people in the United States constitute an oppressed nation.[73] Under conditions of imperialism, the struggles of oppressed nations are objectively revolutionary. There is no contradiction between national and proletarian struggles. The liberation of oppressed nations, overthrow of imperialism, and achievement of socialism are interdependent, each requiring the other.

Haywood, after numerous conversations with his friends and comrades at the Lenin School in Moscow, developed a historical analysis to support viewing black people in the United States as an oppressed nation with a right to self-determination. In brief, he argued that African-American history begins in slavery and continues through the Civil War and betrayal of Reconstruction. This betrayal unleashed "counter-revolutionary terror, including the massacre of thousands of Blacks."[74] Denied the land that should have been theirs had the plantations been confiscated and broken up, black people were reduced again to conditions of near chattel slavery. Imperialism, the stage of capitalism characterized by monopolies, trusts, and financial oligarchy, "froze" black people into their "landless, semi-slave" position, "blocked the road to fusion of Blacks and whites into one nation on the basis of equality and put the final seal of the special oppression of Blacks."[75] Imperialism and racist oppression thus produced those conditions in the South under which black people across the United States became a subject nation. Haywood writes: "They are a people set apart by a common ethnic origin, economically interrelated in various classes, united by a common historical experience, reflected in a special culture and psychological makeup."[76] Their national territory is the Black Belt, where they constitute a majority.

Those comrades who considered African Americans to be an oppressed racial minority took any expression of black nationalism to be reactionary, a diversion from the primary struggle of organizing blacks as workers. They saw "'pure proletarian' class struggle as the sole revolutionary struggle against capitalism."[77] Haywood reported that black comrades from CPUSA offered some of the most vehement criticisms of the idea that black people constituted an oppressed national minority. Rejecting the claim that black people were oppressed as a nation, James Ford argued that there was no systemic economic separation between white people and black people, only racial differences of skin color. Otto Hall (Haywood's brother) said that class interests so divided black people that they could not be considered a national entity and, besides, their primary goal was assimilation.

The second issue in the debate over the Black Belt thesis concerned political tactics and followed closely from the debate over nation versus race. Haywood argued that the emphasis on racial prejudice not only fails to grasp the revolutionary nature of national liberation struggles for self-determination (which Lenin had already articulated) but also fails to provide a position from which to combat white chauvinism in the party and among the white working class. Haywood was particularly concerned that his black comrades in the United States separate racism "from its socio-economic roots, reducing the struggle for equality to a movement against prejudice."[78] To emphasize race rather than nation, he contended, is to "downgrade the revolutionary nature of the Black struggle for equality."[79] Such an emphasis required no radical change (such as land reform and democratic power in the South). It resulted in a bourgeois assimilationist struggle against prejudice and an effort to bring black and white workers together. In contrast, as Haywood explained, the self-determination line

> established that the Black freedom struggle is a revolutionary movement in its own right, directed against the very foundations of U.S. imperialism, with its own dynamic pace and momentum, resulting from the unfinished democratic and land revolutions in the South. It places the Black liberation movement and the class struggle of the U.S. workers in their proper relationship as two aspects of the fight against the common enemy—U.S. capitalism. It elevates the Black movement to a position of equality in that battle.[80]

With this line, the Communist Party would no longer make the mistake of subordinating the black struggle to the class struggle. Instead, the party would have to educate white workers about the revolutionary role of the black liberation struggle. As an article in the *Daily Worker* instructed, "It is the duty of the Communist Party of the U.S.A. to mobilize and rally the broad masses of the white workers for active participation in this struggle."[81] White comrades would have to make black struggle their own—anything less would be a betrayal of the revolution.

Against those who treated black self-determination in the Black Belt as a formula for separatism, Haywood demonstrated its function in building unity. The class consciousness of white workers could only be race consciousness—white chauvinism—if they were not fully committed to the abolition of race hatred, Jim Crow, lynching, prejudice, and "even indifference" to the Negro struggle.[82] Within the party, race prejudice would have to be weeded out and eliminated, "fought with the utmost energy."[83] As Mark Solomon observes, the self-determination line committed the party to fighting for the right of black people "to be free to control the political and social lives of their communities"; at the same time, it redefined "the conception of black-white cooperation on the basis of new power relationships among equals."[84]

The Black Belt thesis put the black comrade in the position of ego ideal, providing the perspective all comrades would have to take toward themselves and their actions. As Solomon writes, "For the dedicated Communist there was no escape from excruciating self-examination."[85] White comrades had to see themselves from a new perspective—not simply that of being equals on the same side in the class struggle but of being equals on the same side of a national liberation struggle, equals fighting against the oppression of a national minority. Were their actions ones that a black comrade would find laudable? Trust? The *Daily Worker* noted that "Every member of the Party must bear in mind" the bitterness and distrust of the oppressed, colonized, and weak masses toward the proletariat of oppressor nations.[86] The party undertook focused work to confront white chauvinism—a campaign of self-criticism, the cultivation of black leaders, mass public trials, and expulsions. It amped up its organizing and recruitment efforts among African Americans. It engaged in what Solomon calls "a frenzy of struggle for equality and black liberation."[87] Some organizers in the US South "criticized purges of racially prejudiced whites."[88] The party took the view that, even if the effect was political isolation in the South, any concession to segregation "would validate racism and sacrifice blacks' trust in white radicals."[89]

The comrade is a generic figure for the political relation between those on the same side. It is characterized by sameness, equality, and solidarity. But what does this mean under conditions of racial capitalism, of a capitalism anchored in white supremacy? It means the active confrontation with and rejection of these conditions in a recomposition of equality and solidarity. The Communist Party's commitment to black self-determination in the Black Belt exemplifies this sort of comradeship. It was utopian, a scandalous insistence that a large area of the southern United States belonged to African Americans because they had built it, their work made it, and their historic experience of capture—in the hold, under the lash, re-enslavement, lynching, and Jim Crow—engendered a national psychology that expressed itself as a collective longing for freedom. The Black Belt slogan refused to let this experience and this longing be subordinated to class struggle or reduced to the abolition of discrimination. The whole Jim Crow capitalist system had to come down.

That anyone but not everyone can be comrade, a thesis I defend in chapter three, means that race does not determine who is a comrade. Comradeship demands the elimination of racism. For a while, the Communist Party was feverishly invested in this process, in ways that sometimes "degenerated into fantastic accusations" and sometimes were manipulated in intraparty machinations. The frequent and repeated accusations, trials, and expulsions, however, gave rise to the sense that racism would never be eradicated from the party.[90] The intense longing for justice and enthusiasm comrades brought to the struggle for black liberation inspired a critical impulse that turned in on itself with a ferocity that seemed to expose comradeship as an impossible ideal. Some criticize the party for its inability to eradicate racism, in the form of white chauvinism, from its ranks. But this criticism can never reach the intensity of the critique the party waged against itself, as I explore further in chapter four.

The Negativity of Comrade

The worry that the comrade is masculine and white arises out of the suspicion that it is stained by a certain positive content. Rather than understood as the figure for a relation that encompasses anybody but not everybody, comrade is treated as the image of a single person, a person that cannot not be gendered and raced (as if the white male has no race or gender). I've addressed this concern by drawing out some of the ways the comrade in the communist tradition—particularly in CPUSA—has not been determined by ascribed identity. Comrade names a relation that exceeds sex and race and that carries with it the expectation that sexism and racism will be combatted and abolished. Abstracting from identities produced through the system of patriarchal racial capitalism, comrade posits a political relation between those who have committed themselves to working together to bring this system down. Liberation from the given enables a new form of relation among equals on the same side of a struggle.

For some contemporary activists, well versed in the politics of identity, often as a result of their own experiences of sexism and racism online and in the movements, there may be some lingering suspicion that comrade isn't formal enough or empty enough, and that no expansive account of the inclusion of positive difference can ever suffice. Attention to the negative dimension of comrade may address this concern. Comrade entails taking a side, rather than refusing to acknowledge and avow the existence of sides. Belonging on the same side lends a generic quality to comradeship: Comrades are indifferent to individual difference, and equal and solidary with respect to their belonging. Comradeship thus requires the dissolution of attachments to the fantasy of self-sufficiency, hierarchy, and individual uniqueness. There is no place for such attachments in the comrade.

The Soviet novelist Andrei Platonov's presentation of comradeship in *Chevengur*, the novel he completed in 1928, illuminates

the comrade's negativity.[91] Far from the disciplined and courageous comrades we associate with Communist parties, Platonov's
comrades are destitute masses who have nothing but each other.
He presents these masses as new arrivals to Chevengur, the village
on the steppe that had achieved communism, writing:

> The new Chevengurians had no joys before them and none
> that they expected, and thus they remained satisfied with that
> which all unpropertied people possess, a life shared with people
> identical for them, companions and comrades for the roads
> through which they pass.[92]

Comrades here are the zero point of possibility, what is left after
everything else is gone, remainders existing in ruins, at the
negative place of beginning. Instead of treating comradeship as
the relation between the Bolsheviks, in his novel Platonov treats
the term comrade like he does communism—both as words existing in an inchoate post-revolutionary vocabulary of rupture,
longing, possibility, and loss. The new world has not arrived, but
there are new words, words which don't quite make sense of the
present, especially for those living on the steppes in the last years of
the Russian civil war. Isabelle Garo writes: "In Chevengur,
communism is the name of a world that does not exist, which
could be constructed and that is already in ruins. It is also a more
subjective than objective reality, or rather a principle of subjectivation."[93] Comrade is the relation necessary for constructing the
new world, a relation present in and as the absence of property,
nationality, and recognizable identity.

Platonov highlights the comradeship of the "miscellaneous" or
"others"—the wandering, propertyless, classless, post-revolutionary,
bastard people. Piled in a heap for warmth at the edge of the town,
these half-naked, starving, orphaned masses are the poorest of
the poor. Their unity is corporeal, the conglomeration of their
multiple international bodies. The Russian word for others or

miscellaneous is *prochie*. Maria Chehonadskih explains that *prochie* was used on early Soviet documents when the class identity of a person was unknowable.[94] *Prochie* are remnants, mistakes, and remainders, proletarianized even of their class identity. The classless *prochie* embody the melancholic moment of revolution.[95] Classes have dissolved. Exploitation has ended. But the new society has yet to be built. The presence of the remaindered others disrupts identitarian logics: Not only are they classless, they lack even nationality; "the torment of life and labor too large had rendered their faces non-Russian."[96] One of Chevengur's Bolsheviks sees in these remainders a glimpse of revolutionary potential:

> That's a class of the first quality that you've got there. You've just got to lead it forward and it won't so much as squeak. This here is your international proletarians. Just look! They aren't Russian, they aren't Armenian, they aren't Tatars . . . they aren't anybody![97]

The others are characterized by loss, by not being anybody at all.[98] The miscellaneous lack a discernible Russian identity—their faces are international, faces from nomads and Mongolians.[99] They lack militancy.[100] They aren't organized, but their comradeship holds the place for something like a future. Their utter destitution has resulted not in atomized individuals isolated in egoistic self-interest but in comradeship as the zero-point of relationality necessary to continue. If communism is possible, it's because the abolition of classes and property leaves comrades to start anew.

The comradeship of the remaindered others is an effect of their destitution. Platonov writes:

> The others had built themselves into self-made people of unknown designation; moreover, this exercise in endurance and inner resources of body had created in the others not only a mind full of curiosity and doubt but also a quickness of

feeling capable of trading eternal bliss for a comrade who was one of them, since this comrade had no father and no property yet was able to make a man forget about both—and within them the others still bore hope, a hope that was confident and successful but sad as loss. What was precise in this hope was this: if the main thing—staying alive and whole—were successfully accomplished, then everything and anything else remaining would be accomplished, even if it were necessary to reduce the world to its last grave.[101]

Comrades let one forget the status that the world gives them—birth, family, name, class. In the absence of these relations, comrades develop a reflex for solidarity that exceeds personal happiness. Commenting on *Chevengur*, McKenzie Wark writes, "The comrades are the ones with which we share life's task of shoring up its impossible relation to a recalcitrant world. All we can share are the same travails, and we are only comrades when we might all share all of them."[102] The shared destitution of those who endure contains hope.

There is a strange opposition between the German and Russian words for comrade. The word in German, *Genosse*, is linked to *geniessen*, to enjoy.[103] It's associated with the shared use or enjoyment of something, with a common relation to property along the lines of a right of use, usufruct.[104] The Russian word for comrade, *tovarish*, comes from *tovar*, which refers to a good for sale, a commodity-thing. The opposition between these word origins seems clear in *Chevengur*. Platonov opposes property and comradeship. Acquisition of property leads to the loss of comradeship; people put their energy into things instead of each other. Platonov writes:

When property lies between people, the people calmly expend their powers on worrying about that property, but when there is absolutely nothing between people, then they begin not to part and to preserve one another from the cold as they sleep.[105]

Comradeship results from the absence of property, not its shared use or enjoyment. As one of the characters in the novel says, "And I say to you that we are all comrades only when there is identical trouble for everybody. As soon as there is bread and property, why you'll never get a man out of it!"[106]

This initial opposition between the German and Russian origins of comrade may be too quick. Platonov's treatment of the *prochie* introduces another kind of property, the collective self-possession of the unpropertied:

> Perhaps these proletarians and miscellaneous served one another as each other's sole possession and worth in life, and thus they looked with such concern at one another, not paying much attention to Chevengur, and carefully kept their comrades free from flies, just as the bourgeoisie had once guarded their homes and livestock.[107]

Having nothing but each other, the miscellaneous nevertheless have something, something to protect and care for. The intimate physicality of swiping away flies gives us a comradeship of the destitute where things (*tovary*) enjoy (*geniessen*) each other; comrades engage in collective self-enjoyment, collective use of the collective. For there to be communism, comrades have to enjoy each other, refusing to let property take the other's place.

In *Chevengur*, the Bolshevik Chepurny worries that women might endanger the preservation of Soviet Chevengur. He thus insists on comrade women, on women whom men will relate to as comrades and not out of desire for sex and progeny:

> Chepurny was ready to welcome any woman to Chevengur so long as her face was darkened by the sadness of poverty and the

old age of work. Then such a woman would be fit only for comradeship and would create no differences in the midst of the oppressed masses, and probably would not evoke that dispersive love consciousness among the lonely Bolsheviks.[108]

Comrade women, like all the remaindered others, are poor, exhausted, sad, and lacking. They are no different from anyone else—that's what makes them comrades.

Platonov's melancholic comradeship gives us insight into the formalization of the lack of identity, nationality, class, and property into a political relation. The comradeship of the others is not an imaginary plentitude of happiness and well-being. On the contrary, it is the minimal degree of relation necessary for endurance, for hope. Comradeship is a necessary condition for communism: the collective of those who enjoy each other refuse to let property take their place. The negation of identity, nationality, class, and property produces something new—a new space of relation that exerts a pressure of its own. The comrade is the zero-level for communism.

Žižek argues that "the zero-level is never 'there,' it can be experienced only retroactively, as the pre-supposition of a new political intervention, of imposing a new order."[109] In *Chevengur*, this is borne out in the way that the miscellaneous are often presented from the perspective of Chepurny's Bolshevik haste to build communism. The narrative voice of the novel deliberately resists localization; it's neither an objective description of facts nor the subjective perception of a single character.[110] Descriptions of the miscellaneous meld into depictions of Chepurny's thoughts and desires and over into his own reflections. For example: "Chepurny sensed how in exchange for the steppe, the houses, the food, and the clothes which the bourgeoisie had acquired for themselves, the proletarians on the mound had each other, because every man has to have something."[111] To Chepurny, those on the mound have not yet appeared as classless others; he sees them as proletarians, as the force that will usher in the future. It's from the position of this communist future—already being built in Chevengur—that the destitution of the remaindered others manifests as comradeship. From the perspective of communism, desolation isn't the end—it's an opening to something we couldn't grasp before; in this instance, the presence of the thing that exists when all is lost: comradeship. The comrade is the zero-level of communism because it designates the relation between those on the same side of the struggle to produce free, just, and equal social relations, relations without exploitation. Their relation is political, divisive. And it is intimate, intertwined with the sense of how desperately each depends upon the other if all are to persevere.

Indifferent to the individual specificities it contains, comrade is a figure of political belonging, term of address, and carrier of expectations for action. As a figure of political belonging, it attends to the relation between those on the same side of a struggle. As a term of address, it refers to those engaged in emancipatory egalitarian struggles for socialism and communism. And, as the following chapter argues, as a carrier of expectations for action, comrade engenders the discipline, joy, enthusiasm, and courage of collective political work.

CHAPTER THREE

Four Theses on the Comrade

MULTIPLE FIGURES OF POLITICAL relation populate the history of political ideas. For centuries, political theorists have sought to explain power and its exercise via expositions of the duties and obligations, virtues and attributes of specific political figures. Machiavelli made the Prince famous (although he wasn't alone in writing for or about princes). There are countless treaties on kings, monarchs, and tyrants. Political theorists have investigated the citizen and foreigner, neighbor and stranger, lord and vassal, friend and enemy. Their inquiries extend into the household: master and slave, husband and wife, parent and child, sister and brother. They include the workplace: schoolmaster and pupil, bourgeois and proletarian. Yet for all these figurations of power, its generation, exercise, and limits, there is no account of the comrade. The comrade does not appear.

The absence of the comrade from US political theory, to use a specific case, could be a legacy of the Cold War. John McCumber's history of the impact of McCarthyism on the discipline of philosophy in the United States notes the twenty-year disappearance of political philosophy from the field.[1] Academic political philosophy only reemerged in 1971 with John Rawls's *Theory of Justice*, a book that subordinated politics to questions of moral justification and secluded actual political and social issues behind a veil of ignorance. But the Cold War can't account for why few socialist and communist theorists produced systematic accounts of the characteristics and expectations of comrades. Perhaps a thorough inquiry into the comrade is missing from "scientific socialism" because socialist and communist thought doesn't offer a political theology of sovereignty or a humanist communion of all humankind. It doesn't provide elaborate origin stories but focuses instead on histories of conflict and struggle. Socialist and communist parties are born out of splits and schisms, simultaneous beginnings and endings of comradeship.

One exception to this general absence of a theory of the comrade can be found in the writing of Bolshevik theorist Alexandra Kollontai. Another exception comes from the Soviet literary writer Maxim Gorky. Neither provides a systematic or analytical explication of the comrade as a figure of political belonging. But they do give us an affective opening into the utopian promise of comradeship.

Thesis One: Comrade names a relation characterized by sameness, equality, and solidarity. For communists, this sameness, equality, and solidarity is utopian, cutting through the determinations of capitalist society.

In her writings on prostitution, sex, and the family from the early years of the Bolshevik revolution, Kollontai presents comradeship and solidarity as sensibilities necessary for building a communist society. She associates comradeship with a "feeling of belongingness," a relation among free and equal communist workers.[2] Under capitalism, workers are not automatically comrades. Capitalism tries to tear them apart and make them competitive, self-interested, and afraid. Communism abolishes these conditions. "In place of the individual and egoistic family, a great universal family of workers will develop, in which all the workers, men and women, will above all be comrades," Kollontai writes.[3] Comrade points to a mode of belonging opposed to the isolation, hierarchy, and oppression of bourgeois forms of relation, particularly of work and the family under capitalism. It's a mode characterized by equality, solidarity, and respect; collectivity replaces egoism and self-assertion. The Russian word for comrade, *tovarish*, is masculine, yet its power is such that it liberates people from the chains of grammar. A Soviet book on literary language published in 1929 gives the example of "comrade sister," a formulation that sounds funny in Russian but evokes the new language and emotions of the revolution.[4]

For Kollontai, comradeship is a core principle of proletarian morality, the key to the "radical re-education of our psyche" under communism. Comradeship engenders new feelings such that people no longer feel themselves unequal and compelled to submit. Now they are "capable of freedom instead of being bound by a sense of property, capable of comradeship rather than inequality and submission."[5]

Maxim Gorky has a short story from the early twentieth century, published in English in 1906 in the *Social Democrat*, that is simply titled "Comrade." The story testifies to the life-giving power of the word *comrade*. Gorky presents comrade as a word that "had come to unite the whole world, to lift all men up the summits of liberty and bind with new ties, the strong ties of mutual respect."[6] The story depicts a dismal, "torturous" city; a city of hostility, violence, humiliation, and rage where the weak submit to the dominance of the strong. In the midst of this miserable suffering, one word rings out: Comrade! The people cease to be slaves. They refuse to submit. They become conscious of their strength. They recognize that they themselves are the force of life.

When people say "comrade," they change the world. One of Gorky's examples is the prostitute who feels a hand on her shoulder and then weeps with joy as she turns around and hears the word *comrade*. With this word, she is interpellated not as a self-commodifying object to be enjoyed by another but as an equal in common struggle against the very conditions requiring commodification. Additional examples are a beggar, a coachman, and young combatants—for all of whom, comrade shines like a star that guides them to the future. Like Kollontai, Gorky associates the word *comrade* with freedom from servitude and oppression, with equality. Like her, he presents the comrade as opposed to capitalism's egoistic exploitation, hierarchy, competition, and misery. And like Kollontai, Gorky links comradeship to a struggle for and vision of a future in which all will be comrades.

Similarly romantic celebrations of relations between comrades infuse the American journal *The Comrade*, published between 1901 and 1905. *The Comrade* was an illustrated monthly publication targeted toward ethically minded, middle-class socialists. It featured poems, short fiction, articles on industry and the conditions of the working classes, translations from European socialists, and autobiographical essays like "How I Became a Socialist." Inspired in part by Walt Whitman's "manly love of comrades," the journal echoes Whitman's homoeroticism, homosociality, and celebratory queerness.[7] Comrade relations are relations of a new type, relations that disrupt the confines of the family, hetero-patriarchy, and binary gender. One of the short stories in the journal, "The Slave of a Slave," is a good example: In the vernacular of the time, the protagonist is a "tomboy" who tries to save a poor woman from her brutal husband and, failing to do so, expresses gratitude that she herself will never be a woman.[8] Today, we might recognize the protagonist as a proud transgender person.

The Comrade featured poems extoling the comrade and comradeship. George D. Herron's "A Song of To-Morrow" dreams "of comrade-love, will fill the world."[9] Edwin Markham's poem, "The Love of Comrades," evokes comrade-bees. An additional Herron poem turns comrade into a prefix: comrade-day, comrade-home, comrade-march, comrade-future, comrade-stars.[10] Russian

constructivist Alexander Rodchenko expands the field of comradeship still further, including comrade objects, comrade things. In
1925, while in Paris he writes:

> The light from the East is not only the liberation of workers, the
> light from the East is in the new relation to the person, to
> woman, to things. Our things in our hands must be equals,
> comrades, and not these black and mournful slaves as they
> are here.[11]

The Soviet writer Andrei Platonov likewise gestures to a comradely
sun and stars, comrade plants, a horse's comradely back.[12] As
Oxana Timofeeva observes, "In his writings, not only humans,
but all living creatures, including plants, are overwhelmed by the
desire for communism."[13]

These examples from Soviet authors and *The Comrade* link
comradeship to a future characterized by equality and belonging,
by a love and respect between equals so great that it can't be
contained in human relations but spans to include insects and
galaxies (bees and stars) and objects themselves.[14] Comrade marks
the division between the world of misery we have and the egalitarian communist world that will be.

Like Soviet revolutionary history and early-twentieth-century
Anglo-US Whitman-inspired homosocialism, the Chinese word
for comrade, *tongzhi*, replaces hierarchical and gendered designa-
tions of relation with an "ideal of egalitarianism and utopianism."[15]
In contemporary Chinese, *tongzhi* also means gay. According to
Hongwei Bao, *tongzhi* is intrinsically queer: It "maps social relations in a new way, a way that opens the traditional family and
kinship structure to relations and connections between strangers
who share the same political views, and it transforms private intimacy into public intimacy."[16] Bao's queer comrades resonate with
Jason Frank's reading of Whitman's ethos of comradeship in his
Calamus poems, where erotic comradely relations destabilize and

overcome "identitarian differences of locality, ethnicity, class, and occupation, sex, race, and sexuality."[17]

Kollontai, Gorky, and their queer comrades inspire the first thesis on the comrade: comrade is a generic and egalitarian—and for communists and socialists, utopian—figure of political relation. The egalitarian dimension of comrade names a relation that cuts through the determinations given by the present. This sense of comrade comes through in the conclusion of *The Wretched of the Earth* as Frantz Fanon appeals repeatedly to his readers as comrades: "Come, comrades, the European game is finally over, we must look for something else" and, in the last line of the book, "For Europe, for ourselves, and for humanity, comrades, we must make a new start, develop a new way of thinking, and endeavor to create a new man."[18] Comrade is the mode of address appropriate to this endeavor. It is egalitarian, generic, abstract, and, in the context of hierarchy, fragmentation, and oppression, utopian.

Communists are not alone in highlighting the utopian dimension of comrade. George Orwell in *Homage to Catalonia* describes Barcelona in 1936, during the Spanish Civil War, in terms of a utopian comradeship. In the revolutionary anarchist setting of Barcelona, he tells us, "Servile and even ceremonial forms of speech had temporarily disappeared. Nobody said 'Senor' or 'Don' or even 'Usted'; everyone called everyone else 'Comrade' and 'Thou,' and said 'Salud!' instead of 'Buenos dias.'"[19]

Today, in a setting that is ever more nationalist and authoritarian, intensely competitive, unequal, and immiserated, in a world of anthropocenic exhaustion, it's hard to recapture the hope, futurity, and sense of shared struggle that were part of an earlier revolutionary tradition. What, then, is comradeship for us? My wager throughout this book is that a speculative-compositive account of comradeship, one that distills common elements from multiple uses of comrade as a mode of address, figure of belonging, and container for shared expectations, can provide us with a view of political relation necessary for the present. Comrades are more than survivors and more than allies. They are those on the same side of a struggle for an emancipated egalitarian world.

Thesis Two: Anyone but not everyone can be a comrade.

Who is the comrade? This question animates Greta Garbo's first scene in Ernst Lubitsch's 1939 film *Ninotchka*.[20] Iranoff, Buljanoff, and Kopalski are three minor Soviet trade officials in Paris to arrange the sale of jewels confiscated from Russian aristocrats. Alas, they give in to bourgeois temptation and become corrupted by the decadence of Parisian wealth, donning tuxedos and drinking champagne. Moscow gets wind of these developments and sends a comrade to straighten the guys out. As the scene opens, Iranoff, Buljanoff, and Kopalski are at the train station to meet the comrade. But who is the comrade? "How can we find somebody without knowing what he looks like?" Kopalski asks. Scanning the passersby, Iranoff thinks he sees the comrade, "That must be the one!" Buljanoff agrees, "Yes. He looks like a comrade." But looks can be deceiving. As they walk toward him, the man they've identified greets someone, "Heil Hitler!" Iranoff shakes his head and declares, "That's not him." Anyone could be their comrade. But not everyone. Some people are clearly not comrades. They are enemies. Iranoff, Buljanoff, and Kopalski can't figure out who their comrade is by looking at them. Identity has nothing to do with comradeship.

As they wonder what they are going to do, they are approached by a woman (Greta Garbo). She announces herself as Nina Ivanova Yakushova, envoy extraordinaire. Kopalski and Iranoff note their surprise that Moscow sent a "lady comrade." Had they known, they would have brought flowers. Yakushova admonishes them, "Don't make an issue of my womanhood. We're here for work all of us." That she is a woman is to be disregarded. Again, identity has nothing to do with comradeship—it's about work, the work of building socialism.

That anyone but not everyone can be a comrade accentuates how comrade names a relation that is at the same time a division. Comradeship is premised on inclusion and exclusion, anyone but not everyone can be a comrade. It is not an infinitely open or flexible relation but one that presupposes division and struggle. There is an enemy. But unlike Carl Schmitt's classic account of the political in terms of the intensity of the antagonism between friend and enemy, comradeship doesn't concern the enemy. The fact of the enemy, of struggle, is the condition or setting of comradeship but it does not determine the relation between comrades. Comrades are those on the same side of the division. With respect to this division, they are the same. Their sameness is that of those who are on the same side. To say comrade is to announce a belonging, and the sameness that comes from being on the same side.

This sameness appears not simply in the relation between party comrades but also in the military expression "comrade in arms." Comrade in arms designates those who fight on the same side against an enemy, another military, or another set of comrades in arms. In his introduction to *The Wretched of the Earth*, Jean-Paul Sartre writes that "every comrade in arms represents the nation for every other comrade. Their brotherly love is the reverse side of the hatred they feel for you."[21] Sartre's slide into the language of brotherhood brings out the ethnic and blood underpinnings of the nation that Schmitt's term "friend" occludes. Sartre alerts us not only to comrades in arms' common relation to the enemy (the hated, the one to be killed), not only to how comrades in arms are those on the same side, but also to the distinction between the comrade in arms and the comrade as a figure of belonging in the socialist and communist political tradition: the solidarity of comrades in the latter sense is not an inverted hatred. As we saw with Kollontai and Gorky, it's a response to fragmentation, hierarchy, isolation, and oppression. In their being on the same side, comrades confront and reject fragmentation, hierarchy, isolation, and oppression with the egalitarian power of belonging.

To reiterate: That anyone but not everyone can be a comrade highlights how comradeship designates a relation and a division— us and them—a political relation but one that is not the same as the relation between friend and enemy, a relation Schmitt presents as an absolute and exclusive state relation. Instead, there is a space of possibility: Anyone can be a comrade, but not everyone. And, there is a space of non-belonging: That you are not my comrade does not mean that you are necessarily my enemy. You may be a bystander, someone politically disengaged, an ally with interests of your own that temporarily overlap with mine, someone who might later come to be a comrade.

Generic, Not Unique

The relation between comrades is not a kinship relation. One is not born a comrade. "Comrade" designates a relation that differs from that between brothers, sisters, parents and children, spouses, or cousins. Kin may and do oppose each other politically; we may be related by blood without sharing a politics. The same holds true for marriage. People can be spouses without being comrades. Conversely, Frida Kahlo famously said of Diego Rivera, whom she married twice, "Diego is not anybody's husband and never will be, but he is a great comrade."[22]

In her history of the British labor movement, *Comrade or Brother?*, Mary Davis observes, "Comradeship builds on fraternity but transcends it."[23] The ease of calling someone "brother" in predominately male unions expresses solidarity yet also gestures to challenges labor has faced with respect to race and gender. To address another as "comrade" is not the same as addressing them as "brother" or "sister," which immediately require assigning a gender identity. Brother and sister rely on a familial imaginary, whether that of the nuclear or extended family or the humanist brotherhood or family of man. Unlike the familial versions, where rivalry underlies the relation between brothers or sisters and a desire to overturn, replace, and perhaps possess or devour infuses the child's relation with its parents, comrade denotes a flat equality, sameness, impersonality, and reciprocity. Desire is not to outdo or replace but to support and be supported, not to let down and not to be let down. Desire is for collectivity.

Just as the relationship between comrades is not mediated by blood or marriage, it is not mediated by inheritance, a constituent feature of the state's investment in kinship. Rather than passing on property and privilege, comrade cuts against them, disrupting their hierarchies with an insistence on equality and mutual need. In *Chevengur*, Chepurny insists on the difference between comrades and brothers:

> Comrades . . . Prokofy called you brothers and a family, but that's a direct lie, because all brothers have a father and we are the many who from the beginning of life have had distinct fatherlessness. We're not brothers, we are comrades. After all, you've come here as you are, and we are each other's goods and valuables, since we have no other movable or unmovable property.[24]

The passage presents comradeship as a relation among the disinherited, the propertyless "bastard people" who have nothing but each other.[25] Familial relations involve property, possession, and the transmission of blood, name, and position. Comradeship is a material relation among those who need each other because they have nothing else, as I explore in chapter two. Chepurny, the head of Chevengur's Revolutionary Action Committee, says, "Property is just ongoing benefit, but comrades are a necessity. Without them, you can't conquer a thing and you end up being a shit yourself."[26] Indeed, throughout the novel, Platonov opposes property and comrades. Criticized for lacking "qualifications or consciousness," a character responds, "We haven't got anything at all . . . The only thing we have left is people, which is why we've got comradeship."[27] Concentrated engagement with others emerges among those unconcerned with property because they have none. Conversely, individuals who think themselves self-sufficient turn their attention to property. Toward the novel's end, Platonov writes, "He forgot how to need people, and then he began to collect property in the place of comrades."[28] The relation between comrades differs from kinship relations because comrades need each other; families are stuck with each other.

Likewise, the comrade is not the neighbor.[29] Living near someone does not make that person your comrade. We may be part of the same locality, the same community, tribe, or neighborhood without being comrades. Comradeship does not designate a spatial relation or an obligation stemming from proximity or shared sociality. When associated with communists, comrade points to political movement, mobility, motion, rootless cosmopolitanism, and internationalism. This nonlocalizability is part of what makes the comrade suspect—comrades may well have tighter relations with those who are far away than they do with those who are right next door.

The comrade is also not the same as the neighbor understood in an ethical sense. "Love thy comrade as thyself" makes no sense: Comrades don't love themselves as uniquely special individuals. They subordinate their individual preferences and proclivities to their political goals. Comrades' relation to each other is outward-facing, oriented toward the project they want to realize, the future they want to bring into being. They cherish one another as shared instruments in common struggle; comrades are a necessity. Žižek presents the neighbor as pure Otherness, "the impenetrable abyss beyond any symbolic identity."[30] In contrast, the comrade is a generic figure, a figure of sameness, the symbolic identity that attends to those belonging to the same side. Žižek notes how, for Lacan, the subject is divided, the empty subject of enunciation and "the symbolic features which identify it in or for the big Other (the signifier which represents it for other signifiers)."[31] The disturbing dimension of the comrade for those who are not comrades is the apparent collapse of these two dimensions. The comrade seems to be nothing but this symbolic identity; the point of enunciation is occupied by the big Other of the party. In *The Morning Breaks: The Trial of Angela Davis*, Bettina Aptheker cites US philosopher (and former Communist) Sidney Hook's claim that a Communist is "by definition incapable of critical analysis and independent judgment, and [is] therefore professionally incompetent."[32] This argument was used by the University of California Board of Regents in an attempt to get Davis fired from her position teaching philosophy at UCLA on the grounds that she was a member of the Communist Party. The attempt failed.

In the sense that comrade names a relation that is generic, equalizing, and open to any but not all, another mode of political membership might seem comparable: the citizen. But while citizenship is a relation mediated by the state, comradeship exceeds the state. It does not take the state as its frame of reference. Comrade does not designate everyone born or residing in a specific territory. One finds comrades all over the world. The early twentieth-century US socialist magazine titled *The Comrade* is interesting on this score as it collects letters, speeches, articles, and other sorts of writing by European socialists. Even as the new US socialists are not yet part of an "International," they emphasize and affiliate with an international political movement. Comrade's rupture of citizen also manifests when we note how the state fears that communists are traitors, people with loyalties to an organization that aims to overthrow the state. In the United States during the Cold War (and still today in right-wing rhetoric), comrade was used sarcastically and derogatorily to accentuate the dangerous otherness of communists. Comrade and citizen can thus stand in an antagonistic relation to each other as the discipline of the comrade is substituted for the law of the state.

When we think of the state in terms of sovereignty, and the concept of the political associated with sovereignty in Schmitt's terms of the distinction between friend and enemy, we can see what makes comradeship so threatening to the state: Comradeship undermines the practical identification of friend and enemy.[33] It disrupts this identification with new ties—as well as with masks and disguises, as I explore below. Comrade rejects the state's logic of identification (papers, policing) and affirms something more ambiguous—anyone could be a comrade.

The relation between comrades is not the same as the relation between friends. This is a crucial point today given the problems in left milieus that can seem exclusive and cliquish. People who would otherwise be on the same side may not come together because closed and unwelcoming friendship groups prevent them from feeling a sense of commonality and belonging. Conversely, personal animosities that destroy friendships can undermine the political work of comrades. Claudio Lomnitz's *The Return of Comrade Ricardo Flores Magón* illustrates the point. Lomnitz describes the lifeworld of the Partido Liberal Mexicano, a transnational network of revolutionary libertarian communists operating in Mexico and the United States and engaging in the Mexican Revolution. Mexican emigres and exiles living in the United States intertwined political work and the work to survive under capitalist conditions. Devoting everything to their cause, some comrades opened themselves up to the opportunism of the less committed, to the exploitation of those who prioritized making their own way in the United States. Tensions around sharing and work, politics and commitment, bled into a suspicion of infiltrators. Lomnitz writes:

> If a comrade was thought to be opportunistic and had personal ambitions, that person could be prone to selling out and maybe even to selling out his comrades. For this reason, the line between personal dislikes and suspicions of treason could get thin, and work was required to keep them distinct.[34]

Comrades may be friends but friendship and comradeship are not the same.[35] We see this most clearly when friendships fray. Personal dislike does not mean that the person is not a comrade. In tight associations, comrade and friend relations blur and overlap. Maintaining the difference and the distance between them takes work, important work. Comradeship requires a degree of alienation from the needs and demands of personal life to which friends must attend.

We learn from Aristotle's *Nicomachean Ethics* that friendship is a direct relation between two people for the benefit of each other. It's a relationship anchored in the person, for the benefit or excellence of the individual. In his reading of Aristotle on friendship, Jacques Derrida emphasizes the "individual singularity" of friendship. "One must prefer *certain* friends."[36] Friends are chosen, selected, on the basis of their excellence, goodness, and virtue. One can only have a small number of friends—there isn't time to devote to more. For Derrida, this counting marks the "becoming-political" of friendship. Friendship isn't originally or necessarily political.[37] Comradeship's egalitarian assertion, in contrast, is intrinsically political: Comrades are bound together in ways that set them apart, that make them a party. Collectivity replaces the individual singularity of friendship. One doesn't choose one's comrades. That one doesn't choose one's comrades does not mean that comrades are not chosen. Nor does it mean they are uncountable. Rather the choosing and counting are matters of political organization; the building up, training, and distributing of forces. One doesn't choose one's comrades. The collective does. In contrast to the narrow exclusivity of friendship, comradeship is broad—bees and stars, someone previously unknown now revealed as a comrade. Comradeship extends from intimate relations all the way to relations with those we don't know personally at all. Anyone can be a comrade, whether or not they like me, whether or not they are like me.

In a couple of places in *Incognegro*, Frank Wilderson gestures to the difference between comrades and friends. He describes the long hours discussing politics and literature with Trevor, a white South African who was his student as well as comrade in an underground MK unit. Wilderson writes, "I once told Trever that he was the best friend I'd ever had." Trevor responds that he doesn't have friends. "Only comrades."[38] Wilderson says that he doesn't know what to make of this. We might consider that Trevor was rejecting the preferential singularity of friendship, a relation that dwells apart from politics. The absorbing work of political struggle creates its own intimacies, its own attachments and intensities. Comrades are bound through their work toward a common goal, not through something merely personal. Wilderson reports another discussion, this one with his first wife, Khanya, a black South African. Khanya says, "You have many White friends . . . but you hate them all."[39] Comradeship abstracts from the specifics of individual lives, from the uniqueness of lived experience. Friendship doesn't. Wilderson's friends remain white; he remains black. He can hate the whiteness of his friends, and his friends for their whiteness, in a way that is deeply personal, wrapped up in life and being. Comradeship is different—it's about the politics, the struggle, the discipline of common work, and the deep sense of connection and accountability that results.

The distinction between the comrade and the friend also points to an inhuman dimension of the comrade: Comradeship has nothing to do with the person or personality in its specificity; it's generic. Comradeship abstracts from the specifics of individual lives to consider how these specifics might contribute to collective goals. What matters is not the uniqueness of a skill or experience but its utility for party work. In this sense, the comrade is liberated from the determinations of specificity, freed by the common political horizon. Ellen Schrecker makes this point in her magisterial account of anticommunism in the United States. During the McCarthy period of communist persecution, there was a common assumption that "all Communists were the same."[40] Communists were depicted as puppets, cogs, automatons, robots, even slaves. In the words of "one of the McCarthy era's key professional witnesses," people who became communists were "no longer individuals but robots; they were chained in an intellectual and moral slavery that was far worse than any prison."[41] The truth underlying the hyperbolic claims of anticommunism is the genericity of the comrade, of comrade as a disciplined and disciplining relation that exceeds personal interests. Comradeship isn't personal. It's political.

The "other relations"—kin, neighbor, citizen, friend—index degenerations of comradeship, errors that comrades make when they substantialize comradeship via race, ethnicity, nationality, and personality. We see this substantializing error in Italian uses of comrade (*camerata*) as a term of address. In Italian, the literal translation of comrade is a fascist political name. Similarly, the German *Kamerad* has a strong military connotation. Yet these substantializations are clear degenerations: the fascist cannot say that anyone can be a comrade. Italian leftists thus use *compagno/compagna*. German socialists and communists use *Genosse/Genossin*. *Genosse* comes from the old German *ginôoz* and *ginôzo*, which designate the shared enjoyment or use of something, cooperative ownership or shared right of use, as I explain in chapter two.[42] Back to my point: the emancipatory egalitarian energy of comrade, its life-giving capacity and ability to map social relations in a new way, is a product of its genericity: anyone but not everyone can be a comrade. When comradeship bleeds into nationality, ethnicity, or race; when it is mistaken for a relation that is supposed to benefit an individual; and when it is equated with relations mediated by the state, the cut of the generic is lost.

Thesis Three: The Individual (as a locus of identity) is the "Other" of the comrade.

Comrade designates a relation, not an individual identity. A 1925 obituary in *Pravda* eulogizes the deceased: "Comrade Nesterenko had no personal biography and no personal needs."[43] The film *Ninotchka* shows that an issue should not be made of the comrade's womanhood; all have work to do. On the left, comrade is a term of address that attaches to proper names—Comrade Yakushova. The proper name carries the individual identity; the term of address asserts a sameness. Following a large, daylong demonstration against white supremacists, a comrade of mine joyfully noted, "We don't even need to know each other's names—we're comrades." "Comrade" takes the place of "Sir," "Madam," and "Citizen." It negates the specificity of a determined title, a title that inscribes differentiation and hierarchy, and replaces it with a positive insistence on an equalizing sameness. At the same time, comrade requires a decision and inscribes a cut. Because not everyone is a comrade, calling someone a comrade marks a divide: Are you with us or not?

Oxana Timofeeva emphasizes that in comradeship identity vanishes.[44] She gives the example of the masquerade used by Bolsheviks undercover. Anyone could be under that mustache. Schrecker provides a further example, a statement from General Herbert Brownell, attorney general under President Dwight D. Eisenhower. Brownell's suspicions of Communists were heightened because, in his words, it was "almost impossible to 'spot' them since they no longer use membership cards or other written documents which will identify them for what they are."[45] In these examples, it's the generic comrade who appears, masking an individual person, yet one of many; it could be anyone. Schrecker quotes Herbert Philbrick, an undercover informer: "Anyone can be a Communist. Anyone can suddenly appear as a Communist Party member—close friend, brother, employee or even employer, leading citizen, trusted public servant."[46]

Bertolt Brecht's cantata *The Measures Taken* (*Die Massnahme*) similarly explores the antithetical relation between individual identity and the comrade. Four agitators are on trial before a party central committee (the Control Chorus) for the murder of their young comrade. The agitators describe how they went undercover in order to reach Chinese workers they are trying to organize. Each agitator had to efface their identity, to be "nameless and without a past, empty pages on which the revolution may write its instructions."[47] Each agitator, including the young comrade, agreed to fight for communism and be themselves no longer. They all put on Chinese masks, appearing to be Chinese rather than German and Russian. Instead of following instructions and carrying out the plan, however, the young comrade repeatedly substituted his judgment for that of the party, encouraging action before the time was right. He could see with his own two eyes that "misery cannot wait," so he tore up the party writings. He tore off and up his mask. He sought to hasten the revolution and his impetuosity set the movement back. Forced to flee from the Chinese authorities, the agitators and the young comrade raced to escape the city. The agitators realized that since the young comrade had become identifiable, they had to kill him. The young comrade agreed. The four agitators shot him, threw him into a lime pit that would burn away all traces of him, and returned to their work.

Comrades are multiple, replaceable, fungible. They are elements in collectives, even collections. As I mention in chapter one, in several Romance languages *comrade* originated as a term for those who share a room or travel together. To be a comrade is to share a sameness with another with respect to where you are both going. Incidentally, these elements of sameness and collectivity point to the difference between the comrade and the militant. The militant is a single figure fighting for a cause. That one is a militant tells us nothing about that one's relation to others. The militant expresses political intensity, not political relationality.

In the transition to capitalism that took place in Russia post-1991, the term comrade started to become discredited. Alla Ivanchikova tells me that this was a political struggle, fought through etymology. New etymologies sought to depoliticize and mock the term. They highlighted its origin in the word *tovar*, or commodity, a good for sale.[48] Ivanchikova explained that "this clearly serves the purpose of showing that underneath all talk of 'comradery' there are monetary and market relations that rule the day. Any comrade (*tovarish*) is a commodity (*tovar*), if you pay the right price."[49] Counter-etymologies insist that the word *tovar* is much older than its reference to a commodity or good produced for sale. *Tovar* derives from an ancient word for military camp, *tovarŭ*.[50] Soldiers called themselves comrades.

Underlying this etymological warfare is an assumption of sameness. Interchangeability, whether between soldiers, commodities, schoolchildren, travelers, or party members, characterizes the comrade. As with puppets, cogs, and robots, commonality arises not out of identity, not out of who one is, but out of what is being done—fighting, circulating, studying, traveling, or being part of the same apparatus. Political comrades are those on the same side. Communist comrades are those struggling to emancipate society from capitalism and create new egalitarian modes of free association and collective decision making for common benefit.

For anticommunists, the instrumentalism of comrade relations appears horrifying. Combined with the machinic impersonality and fungibility of comrades, the fact that relations between comrades are produced for an exterior purpose, that they are means rather than ends in themselves, seems morally objectionable. This objection fails to acknowledge the specificity of comradeship as a political relation, as being on the same side of struggle. It omits the way political work focuses on ends beyond the individual and so necessarily requires collective coordination. It presumes a totalizing politics that subsumes all relations rather than recognizing an abstract politics liberated or alienated from specific social relations. And it contracts the space of meaning into self-relations, as if abstracted generic relations among those faithful to a political truth could only be the result of manipulation.

In an interview with Vivian Gornick, a former member of CPUSA described his life of meetings, actions, May Day parades, selling the *Daily Worker*, and endlessly discussing Marx and Lenin as "beyond good or bad," as "sweeping, powerful," and "intense, absorbing, filled with a kind of comradeship I never again expect to know."[51] He saw himself as useful, living in the service of a struggle of world historical significance. His actions were not individual; they were moments in collective struggle, instances through which the collective power of the party could appear.[52] Precisely because he was engaged with others in a common purpose, the comrade experienced deep political meaning. We have to reject the bourgeois fiction that intimacy depends on personal disclosure, individual experience, or the way a singular person feels about people and events. There are other intimacies of common work and shared purpose: preparing the newspaper, making the banners, planning an action, knocking on doors.

Thesis Four: The relation between comrades is mediated by fidelity to a truth. Practices of comradeship materialize this fidelity, building its truth into the world.

By the end of the nineteenth century, comrade was a prominent term in socialist circles. Kirsten Harris finds the first socialist evocation of comradeship written in English to be in the journal *Justice* in 1884. Some English socialists were inspired by Whitman's vision of the deep fellowship and interconnectedness of comrades. It spoke to their sense that the relation among those in socialist struggle, as well as in the new society to come, was based on more than brotherhood (an identification that was prominent in the labor movement) or fraternity (an ideal anchored in universal kinship that acquired currency during the French

Revolution). The term's military background rendered comrade an able carrier of the ideal of a "bond that is forged when a common cause is fought side by side."⁵³ The English embrace of Whitman resonated with US socialists. In a short essay in *The Comrade* published in 1903, W. Harrison Riley recounted some of his encounters with Marx (whom he said "was as good to look at as to listen to" and "well built and remarkably good looking"). Riley observed that "the Internationalists addressed each other as 'Citizen,' but I disliked the designation and frequently substituted Whitman's greeting, 'Comrade.'"⁵⁴

Riley's gesture to Whitman notwithstanding, "comrade" was already part of the political vocabulary of German socialists.⁵⁵ In his writings, Marx used the term in a variety of ways, including as a designation for those in the same political party, those sharing the same politics. "Party" referred not just to a formal organization but to broader political movement. In his well-known letter to Kugelmann on the Paris Commune, Marx praises "our heroic Party comrades in Paris."⁵⁶ The Communards referred to here are not Marx's comrades in a specific party but in the party understood in the "broad historical sense."⁵⁷ They were all on the same side, that of "real people's revolution."⁵⁸ In a text for the International Workingmen's Association written in 1866, Marx draws out this political dimension of comrade: "It is one of the great purposes of the Association to make the workmen of different countries not only *feel* but *act* as brethren and comrades in the army of emancipation."⁵⁹ More than union brothers involved in local and national struggles, members of the IWA would be comrades in international political struggle, fighting on the side of their class in the struggle of labor against capital. Their common condition as workers needed to become the basis for a common politics, a shared political orientation. As comrades in an army of emancipation, they would combine and generalize their efforts. No longer would the differences between foreign and domestic workers be able to be used against them. As comrades, they were all the same. G. W. Pabst's

1931 film *Kameradschaft* depicts just such a version of the comrade-ship of workers. Separated above ground by national borders, French and German miners work together below ground to rescue their comrades after explosions have collapsed parts of the mine. As miners and as workers, they are united by a bond greater than the nationalities that separate them.

The idea that comrades are those who belong to the same side of a political struggle leads to the fourth thesis: The relation between comrades is mediated by fidelity to a truth; practices of comrade-ship materialize this fidelity. The "same side" points to the truth comrades are faithful to—the political truth that unites them—and the fidelity with which they work to realize this truth in the world. "Belonging" invites attention to the expectations, practices, and affects that being on the same side generates.

The notions of truth and fidelity at work here come from Alain Badiou. In brief, Badiou rejects the idea of truth as a proposition or judgment, arguing instead that truth is a process. The process begins with the eruption of something new, an event. Because an event changes the situation, breaks the confines of the given, it is undecidable in terms of the given; it is something entirely new. Badiou argues that this undecidability "induces the appearance of a *subject* of the event."[60] This subject isn't the cause of the event. It's an effect of or response to the event, "the decision to *say* that the event has taken place." Grammar might seduce us into rendering this subject as "I." We should avoid this temptation and recognize the subject as designating an inflection point, a response that extends the event. The decision that a truth has appeared, that an event has occurred, incites a process of verification, the "infinite procedure of verification of the true," in what Badiou calls an "exercise of fidelity."[61] Fidelity is a working out and working through of the truth, an engagement with truth that extends out into and changes the world. We should recognize here the unavoid-ably collective dimension of fidelity: in the political field, verification is a struggle of the many.

Peter Hallward draws out some implications of Badiou's conception of truth. First, it is subjective. Those faithful to an evental truth involve themselves in working it out, exploring its consequences.[62] Second, fidelity is not blind faith; it is rigorous engagement unconcerned with individual personality and incorporated into the body of truth that it generates. Hallward writes:

> Fidelity is, by definition, ex-centric, directed outward, beyond the limits of a merely personal integrity. To be faithful to an evental implication always means to abandon oneself, rigorously, to the unfolding of its consequences. Fidelity implies that, if there is truth, it can be only cruelly indifferent to the private as such. Every truth involves a kind of anti-privatization, a subjective collectivization. In truth, "I" matter only insofar as I am subsumed by the impersonal vector of truth—say, the political organization, or the scientific research program.[63]

The truth process builds a new body. This body of truth is a collective formed to "work for the consequences of the new" and this work, this collective, disciplines and subsumes the faithful.[64] Third, collectivity does not imply uniformity. The infinite procedure of verification incorporates multiple experiments, enactments, and effects.

Badiou writes, "An organization lies at the intersection between an Idea and an event. However, this intersection only exists as process, whose immediate subject is the political militant."[65] We should amend this statement by replacing *militant* with *comrade*. Comrade highlights the "discipline of the event," the way that political fidelity cannot be exercised by a solitary individual— hence, the Marxist-Leninist emphasis on the unity of theory and practice, the barren incapacity of each alone. Comrade also affirms the self-abandonment accompanying fidelity to a truth: its vector, its unfolding, is indifferent to my personal experiences and inclinations. For communists, the process of truth has a body and that body is the party, in both its historical and formal sense. Already in *Theory of the Subject*, Badiou recognizes the necessity of a political body, the party as the "subject-support of all politics."[66] He writes:

> The party is the body of politics, in the strict sense. The fact that there is a body by no means guarantees that there is a subject . . . But for there to be a subject, for a subject to be found, there must be the support of a body.[67]

As a figure of political belonging, the comrade is a faithful response to the evental rupture of crowds and movements, to the egalitarian discharge that erupts from the force of the many where they don't belong, to the movement of the people as the subject of politics.[68] Comrades demonstrate fidelity through political work; through concerted, disciplined engagement. Their practical political work extends the truth of the emancipatory egalitarian struggle of the oppressed into the world. Amending Badiou (by drawing from his earlier work), we can say that the comrade is not a faithful subject but a political relation faithful to the divided people as the subject of emancipatory egalitarian politics.[69] For us to see the revolutionary people as the subject in the struggles of the oppressed, for their subject to be found, we must be comrades.

In *Ninotchka*, Nina Ivanova Yakushova can't tell who her comrades are by looking at them. The party has told her who to look for, but she has to ask. After Iranoff identifies himself, Yakushova tells him her name and the name and position of the party comrade who authorized her visit. Iranoff introduces Buljanoff and Kopalski. Yakushova addresses each as comrade. But it's not the address that makes them all comrades. They are comrades because they are members of the same party. The party is the organized body of truth that mediates their relationship. This mediation makes clear what is expected of comrades—disciplined, faithful work. Iranoff, Buljanoff, and Kopalski have not been doing the work expected of comrades, which is why Moscow sent Yakushova to oversee them in Paris. That Kopalski says they would have greeted her with flowers demonstrates their *embourgeoisment*, the degeneration of their sense of comradeship. But they are all there for work. Gendered identity and hierarchy don't mediate relations between comrades. The practices of fidelity to a political truth, the work done toward building that truth in the world, do.

The solidarity of comrades in political struggle arises out of the intertwining of truth, practice, and party. It's not reducible to any of these alone. Comrades are not simply those who believe in the same truth—as in, for example, the idea of communism. Their fidelity to a certain truth is manifested in practical work. Work for the realization of a political truth brings people into comradely relation. But carrying out similar tasks in fidelity to the same truth isn't sufficient for comradeship. The work must be in common; no one is a comrade on their own. Practices of comradeship are coordinated, organized. The party is the organization out of which comradeship emerges and that comrade relations produce. It concentrates comradeship even as comradeship exceeds it.

Just as there are four theses on the comrade, so does the comrade have four primary characteristics: discipline, joy, enthusiasm, and courage. If, as I argue in *The Communist Horizon*, communism is a collective desire for collectivity, then comradely discipline functions as its law and language. Discipline—meetings, reports, work, demonstrations, campaigns, "unity of action," carrying out the line—provides the language through which previously inchoate and individual longing becomes collective will. Discipline also provides the impediment that maintains desire: organizing requires planning and postponement. The comrade here is not the same as the militant who might celebrate and pursue the heroic and individualistic propaganda of the deed. As we have already seen with Brecht, the young comrade's impatience botched the whole operation and so his comrades had to kill him.

Comradeship is a disciplining relation: Expectations, and the responsibility to meet them, constrain individual action and generate collective capacity. Comrades learn to push immediate self-interest and the desire for personal comfort or advancement aside for the sake of the party, the movement, and the struggle. Discipline negates and creates. It induces the subordination of personal interest for the sake of producing a new force, a force strong enough to endure the long years of revolutionary struggle and prevail. In the words of one of the Communists Gornick interviewed in *The Romance of American Communism*: "To be involved with people in a political enterprise, to feel that particular comradeship, to watch people becoming in such an atmosphere, that is to feel the world being made anew."[70]

Lenin famously and frequently spoke of the need for discipline in the revolutionary party—rigorous discipline, proletarian discipline, iron discipline, socialist discipline, comradely discipline, and so on. Party discipline generally referred to the expectations of unity in action, free discussion, and criticism.[71] Proletarian, or labor, discipline differed insofar as it pointed to the new organization of labor under socialism, the voluntary organization of class-conscious workers. Rather than being subjected to the will of the bosses, the forces of the market, or the tyranny of the wage, the "conscious and voluntary initiative of the workers" yields new gains in productivity, more advanced techniques of production.[72] The working class demonstrates through proletarian discipline that capitalists and landlords are superfluous. We don't need them. We can—and will—do it ourselves. In each kind of discipline, what matters is that discipline is freely accepted. For Lenin, discipline itself is revolutionary, more revolutionary than the defeat of the bourgeoisie: "for it is a victory over our own conservatism, indiscipline, petty-bourgeois egoism, a victory over the habits left as a heritage to the worker and peasant by accursed capitalism."[73] Through comradely discipline, we make one another stronger. Our commitment to working together toward our common goal works back on us, enabling us to surmount and maybe even abolish those individualist attributes produced by capitalism. We can make mistakes, learn, and change. By recognizing our own inadequacies, we come to understand the need to be generous and understanding toward the shortcomings of others. We develop an appreciation for strengths and talents that we had been unable to see. We become a new kind of collectivity.

One doesn't have to be a Bolshevik to recognize the necessity of revolutionary discipline. In *Homage to Catalonia*, Orwell says that "'revolutionary' discipline depends on political consciousness—on an understanding of *why* order must be obeyed."[74] The explanation for a given task, which generates a shared understanding of the task's importance, is one of the ways that equality replaces hierarchy. If we are on the same side, if we share the same goals, we have to coordinate our actions to realize them. As comrades, we take on tasks voluntarily; we discipline ourselves because that's what political action requires.

Accompanying comradely discipline is joy, the second characteristic of the comrade. In a pamphlet on Communist *subbotniks*— that is, Saturdays of voluntary labor undertaken during the Civil War—Lenin quotes an article that appeared in *Pravda* celebrating the enthusiastic voluntary work done on the Moscow-Kazan railway:

> When the workers, clerks and head office employees without even an oath or argument, caught hold of the forty-pood wheel tire of a passenger locomotive and, like industrious ants, rolled it into place, one's heart was filled with fervent joy at the sight of this collective effort, and one's conviction was strengthened that the victory of the working class was unshakable . . . When the work was finished those present witnessed an unprecedented scene: a hundred Communists, weary, but with the light of joy in their eyes, greeted their success with the solemn strains of the Internationale.[75]

The joy of discipline is internal and external, felt by comrades and experienced by those who witness how discipline changes the world. Through the intense collectivity that discipline enables, comrades can do the impossible; they are liberated from prior expectations and constraints. Joy accompanies the sense of collective invincibility. *Together we made it happen—and we did it for purposes larger than ourselves.* A CPUSA section organizer describes the power that accrues when people join together as

> the thrill of seeing one become through the other, the idea through the structure, the structure through the action. And the whole of it discipline, each by its own properties, own function, and together, by the grand design that only a disciplined existence could form.[76]

Joy in comradeship testifies to the freedom that discipline affords.

Comrades do their work with enthusiasm, the comrade's third characteristic. They are praised for the energy they bring to their tasks. Describing his years in the Communist Party of Great Britain, Raphael Samuel writes:

> The Party was honeycombed with people to look up to, people you were honoured to meet because they had given their lives to the cause; people of unbroken spirit, "people whom nothing would shake." There were the comrades who set an example to others by their energy and enthusiasm.[77]

In *What Is to Be Done?*, Lenin repeatedly praises the energy of the German Social Democrats, criticizes his economist comrades for their lack of energy, and calls upon his party to increase its energy. In his conversation with Clara Zetkin, Lenin spoke highly of the energy and enthusiasm of the party's women comrades, adding, "I forget for the moment who said: 'One must be enthusiastic to accomplish great things.'"[78] Enthusiasm, energy, is expected of comrades because it is that extra, that surplus benefit of collectivity, which enables them to do more, even to win. What distinguishes comrades from politically minded and hardworking individuals is the energy that accrues to collective work. Because they combine forces, they generate more than each could by working alone. Enthusiasm is the surplus that collective discipline generates.

The fourth attribute of the comrade is courage. We saw at the beginning of this chapter, in the description of Gorky's short story "Comrade," the courage the comrade inspires in those interpellated by it—they become powerful enough to break the chains of servitude, escape the confines of misery, and stand up against oppression. Chinese Communist Party leader Liu Shaoqi describes the revolutionary courage of the Communist as an effect of comradely discipline:

> Having no selfish motives, [the Communist] has nothing to fear. Having done nothing to give himself a guilty conscience, he can lay bare and courageously correct his mistakes and short comings . . . Because he has the courage of righteous conviction, he never fears the truth, courageously upholds it, spreads it and fights for it.[79]

The courage of the comrade is not an individual virtue. It's an effect of discipline, the strength that arises as a result of self-denial in the service of common struggle. Comradely courage includes the capacity for self-criticism, the capacity to admit to being wrong or not knowing and then correct any errors through further study and work. The Bolsheviks linked courage to being steadfast, unwavering, unyielding, and resolute; to the capacity to endure and prevail under enormous hardship. Kollontai's praise for the great women fighters of the October Revolution provides some examples. Commending Lenin's wife, Kollontai writes, "In moments of greatest difficulty and danger, when many stronger comrades lost heart and succumbed to doubt, Nadezhda Konstantinovna remained always the same, totally convinced of the rightness of the cause and of its certain victory."[80] And of another comrade: "Enormous work was done by Varvara Nikolayevna Yakovleva during the difficult and decisive days of the October Revolution in Moscow . . . Many comrades said then that her resolution and unshakable courage gave heart to the wavering and inspired those who had lost heart."[81]

These four attributes of the comrade—discipline, joy, enthusiasm, and courage—characterize the comrade's practical fidelity, the way comrade responds to the egalitarian discharge of the crowd and works to realize and extend this moment as the movement of the revolutionary people. In a critical engagement with Badiou, Žižek proposes "'four fundamental concepts of emancipatory politics': anxiety, courage, terror, enthusiasm."[82] He makes this proposal as a counter to Badiou's early treatment of the subject-effect as a knot of the four concepts anxiety, courage, justice, and superego as well as to Badiou's later substitution of terror for superego.[83] None of these tetrads suffice for a theory of the comrade. The comrade is not a subject; it is a figure of political belonging, term of address, and set of expectations. In the latter sense, it functions as an ideal ego and an ego ideal. My focus here has been on its role as an ego ideal. To the extent that the party is an organized response to an event retroactively attributed to the divided people as its subject, the comrade is an effect, a relational effect, the effect of a truth-event on people's relations to each other, things, and the world.

In *Crowds and Party*, I present the party as a form through which Badiou's subject-effects are intertwined with Elias Canetti's crowd elements—growth, direction, equality, and density. Seeing the people in the crowd, the party gives the crowd a politics and a history, enabling its egalitarian moment to endure. The party does this by concentrating the subject-effects of anxiety, courage, justice, and superego into a transferential site from which they can work back on the collectivity. Transference here is a formal effect of collectivity, not the intervention of an individual person as a leader but the working of the side or party back onto the members.[84] To use Žižek's frame, the four concepts of the party are concentration, endurance, fidelity, and transference. Applied to the party's members, its cadre, the comrades, this set of four concepts yields the attributes of the comrade—discipline, joy, enthusiasm, and courage. As a figure of political belonging, the comrade contains (like a vault or chamber) the effects of the party, of being on the same side, and directs these effects back onto those who share a politics.

What, then, is the problem with Žižek's four fundamental concepts of emancipatory politics—anxiety, courage, terror, and enthusiasm? The short answer is that this politics has no body. The four concepts comprise a disembodied response that consequently lacks the capacity for fidelity and endurance. It lacks relationality. It lacks a means by which to concentrate forces or extend effects. Žižek's four concepts remain spontaneous, descriptive of revolution's atmosphere and of the affective responses that bear witness to the people as their cause. They lack political form.

Terror exemplifies the problem with the disembodiment of Žižek's concepts of emancipatory politics. As a fundamental experience of dislocation or confrontation with an ontological void, the concept of terror is philosophically useful. For activists, organizers, and political theorists, however, the appeal to terror seems like provocation for its own sake, a kind of inauthentic acting out that Žižek himself frequently decries. Terror functions as a placeholder for planned, organized political work (which might include terror as a tactic but does not elevate it to a fundament).

In *Theory of the Subject*, Badiou includes superego as one of four effects of the subject. Nevertheless, even here he associates superego and terror. In his exposition of the relation between anxiety, superego, courage, and justice, Badiou presents anxiety as the name for the "power void," a situation of paralyzed disorder, of "mute and suicidal riots."[85] Unable to tolerate this situation, anxiety calls for its resolution (or, better, anxiety is the excessive, reflexive moment of the void's inability to tolerate itself). Anxiety summons superego to restore order, which occurs through the ferocious extension of law. Law becomes omnipresent, terroristic, spreading the excessive element of anxiety everywhere. Its inner truth as non-law is "set free."[86]

Badiou's explication of superego in terms of the terroristic imposition of the law ignores another "non-law" responsive to the subject that causes it—the discipline of the revolutionary party. Discipline, however, is a necessary supposition of his argument. Badiou argues that the dual moments of subjectivization and subjective process occasion destruction and recomposition, a reordering in light of the new. A *political* response to the intervention of a subject directs, aspirationally, in the sense of steering but more often in the sense of indicating. The response ascribes a retroactive consistency to the subject that instigated it. The communist party is the carrier or body of the political response faithful to the divided people as its subject. As Badiou writes, "For there to be a subject, for a subject to be *found*, there must be the support of a body."[87] The body that enables the subject to be found supplies a political form of non-law that provides another path for anxiety—the path of recomposition in light of the new—in fidelity to the emancipatory egalitarian moment of rupture. In the party, discipline takes the place of law, cutting through the division of law and crime with the expectations comrades have of each other. Rendering the party an organized force, discipline imbues it with the capacity to go beyond law, to act legally or illegally as conditions demand.

Consider the tragic example of the Kronstadt rebellion in 1921. Led by anarchists, Red Navy sailors at the naval fortress called for a third revolution "to overthrow the Bolsheviks and establish Soviet democracy."[88] Some Communists joined them in revolt. After Bolshevik forces defeated the uprising in one of the cruelest battles of the entire civil war, Trotsky justified the Bolsheviks' attack by saying that they had waited "for our blinded sailor-comrades to see with their own eyes where the mutiny led."[89] Isaac Deutscher observes that Trotsky's description of "the crushed rebels as 'comrades' ... intimated that what he celebrated was a morally Pyrrhic victory."[90] This may be true. But it also attests to the ferocity of discipline such that its violations incite a specific kind of fury, one fueled by outrage at betrayal, abandonment, and renegacy. That the rebels were comrades justified the battle's cruel intensity.

The superegoic dimension of discipline also accounts for the ferocity of the party's own inward turns: Its attacks on itself generally exceed and restrain its attacks on the people. At the same time, that superego is channeled through discipline accounts for its creative intensity, the way the party compels comrades to push themselves and each other to do the impossible—and to do it enthusiastically. Discipline thus includes the negativity crucial to Žižek's larger position. Absent the discipline of comrades, the party is nothing, utterly incapable of furthering a political project. Yet, like Badiou, Žižek embraces the substitution of terror for superego, the disembodied spread of non-law over the discipline required to intervene in a revolutionary situation.

Sometimes in psychoanalysis desire appears as a will to transgress. Law supports desire by setting a limit and desire persists so long as the limit is never reached. Comradely discipline modulates transgression into excess, into exceeding the limit, going beyond it, and doing more. The Soviets' over-fulfilled five-year plans are a famous example. We might also add the ways comrades so easily fault themselves for not doing enough. On the one hand, the discipline of expectations, plans, and program provides a barrier—a bit of breathing space or relief from the self-imposed injunction to do more. Yet, in capitalist society, we are constantly enjoined to affirm our unique assessment, our individual opinion, our personal choice, incessantly commanded to differentiate and hierarchicize. Discipline is a challenge. On the other hand, the collective desire for collectivity, as it pushes us to exceed all limits with the urgency of the struggle for justice—and the reality of enemies and counterrevolutionaries—can make discipline feel too constraining. *We must do more! Be more vigilant, more correct!* Disciplinary provisions such as expulsions then become excessive, superegoistic. Comrades become their own worst enemies. The discipline that made them strong, that gave them capacity, destroys what it produced.

In sum, as it requires ongoing self-subordination, denial, and sacrifice, discipline takes on and risks all the excesses of the super-ego. Comrades can never do enough—and they place the demand to do more on themselves. The conceptual advantage afforded by discipline is thus the jettisoning of a radical infatuation with the terror that emancipatory politics may inflect on others and the replacement of that infatuation with the sacrifices emancipatory politics demands of those who seriously undertake it.

Žižek's emphasis on enthusiasm is correct, but as a corollary not to terror but to courage. Žižek argues that enthusiasm forms a couplet with terror as "its immanent reversal." He invokes Kant "for whom the terror at our utter impotence in face of the unleashed violence of some natural power turns into enthusiasm when we become aware of how not even the mightiest natural violence can threaten our autonomy as free moral agents."[91] Žižek emphasizes that terror guarantees enthusiasm's authenticity. Of course, in politics there are never any guarantees. The only way to distinguish between true and false enthusiasm is by effects, results, works. Did enthusiasm enhance the work of the collective? Did it strengthen resolve? Did it make comrades more courageous than they might have otherwise been? Žižek's version too easily devolves into an enthusiasm for terror. In contrast, the comrade accesses a disciplined and joyful politics where enthusiasm generates courage, the courage to adapt to circumstances, to respond at crucial junctures, to retreat to a position of strength, to plan for contingencies, and to recognize that we learn which tactics are correct from the people.

*   *   *

Comrade is more than a term of address. As a figure of political belonging, it's a carrier of expectations for action—the expectations that those on the same side have of each other, expectations that should be understood via Badiou as the "discipline of the event."[92] Obama's joke about Sanders that I recount in chapter one notes one such expectation: you don't distance yourself from your comrades. Kollontai likewise affirms the fact that comradeship connotes more than sharing political beliefs; it has practical impact, effects on what we do. The primary virtue of comrades is solidarity; fidelity is demonstrated through reliable, consistent, practical action. Differences between parties often turn on what comrades can expect of each other, on what it means to be a comrade. Broadly speaking, comrades in most revolutionary socialist and communist parties are expected to engage in the struggles of the oppressed, organize for revolution, and maintain a certain unity of action. Absent expectations of solidarity, comrade as term of an address is an empty signifier. Rather than figuring the political relation mediated by the truth of communism, it becomes an ironic or nostalgic gesture to a past utopian hope.

To demonstrate how the figure of the comrade can be an operator for a politics for those engaged in emancipatory egalitarian struggle, I've offered four theses:

1. Comrade names a relation characterized by sameness, equality, and solidarity. For communists, this sameness, equality, and solidarity is utopian, cutting through the determinations of capitalist society.
2. Anyone but not everyone can be a comrade.
3. The individual (as a locus of identity) is the Other of the comrade.
4. The relation between comrades is mediated by fidelity to a truth. Practices of comradeship materialize this fidelity, building its truth into the world.

The first two theses express the disruptive negativity of comrade. We can think of this disruption as the hail that interpellates the addressee as one among many, as one who is on our side (not on their own and not a superior or subordinate). Transcripts of Communist Party congresses and meetings record people fiercely disagreeing yet affirming that their disagreement is occurring among those who share a politics. They incessantly hail each other as "Comrade." Sometimes this hail is answered in unexpected ways. Consider the tumultuous three-week-long meeting of the first All-Russian Congress of Soviets in Petrograd in June 1917. Divisions between the parties—the Cadets, the Social Revolutionaries, the Mensheviks, and the Bolsheviks—were intensifying. Trotsky began an address with the word "Comrades" and was interrupted by shouts: "'What sort of comrades are we to you?' and 'Stop calling us comrades!' He stopped, and he moved closer to the Bolsheviks."[93] Here, the disruptive negativity of comrade signals the end of one relation and the consolidation of another. Sides are clarified. People know whom they stand with and who stands with them. At any rate, the first two theses index comrade's rejection of a naïve ideological imaginary of everyone in favor of a partisan subjectivation.

The second two theses embody the working back of the side on those who are on it, such that being on the same side produces the comrade relation, composing the expectations comrades have of each other.[94] Comrades put individual identity aside as they work together for justice. Collective desire replaces the fiction that desire can be individual. Of course, this doesn't mean that comrades don't recognize how ascribed identities are vehicles for oppression and discrimination, as I explore in chapter two. Rather, comradeship is a political relation not determined by or beholden to these identities. Comradeship generates new values, intensities, and possibilities. Alienation from the oppressive determinations of capitalism induces the disalienation of collective engagement for a common purpose. Together the four theses articulate a generic political component activated through divisive fidelity to the emancipatory egalitarian struggle for communism. A comrade is one of many fighting on the same side.

In the concluding chapter, I take up the end of comradeship. What happens when you are not my comrade?

Chapter Four

You Are Not My Comrade

I'VE PRESENTED COMRADE AS a mode of address, figure of political belonging, and carrier of expectations. As it gives form to the political relation between those on the same side, comrade promises alienation and fulfillment: liberation from the constraints of racist patriarchal capitalism and a new relation born of collective political work toward an emancipatory egalitarian future. Exceeding a sense of politics as individual conviction and choice, comrade points to expectations of solidarity as indispensable to political action. We show up to meetings we would otherwise miss, do political work we might avoid, and try to live up to our responsibilities to each other. We experience the joy of committed struggle, of learning through practice. We overcome fears that might overwhelm us were we forced to confront them alone. My comrades make me better, and stronger, than I could ever be on my own.

Consider how odd it sounds to use "comrade" as a self-description: "I am a comrade." In stark contrast to "I am an ally," one would never say "I am a comrade." Comrade points immediately to another who is not myself but rather someone who stands together with me in common struggle. It forces the acknowledgement of political belonging: "I have a comrade." There is someone who will swipe the flies from my back. The comrade is the zero-level of communism because it changes our relation to ourselves, each other, and the world. It thereby marks a political relation beyond the friend-enemy binary, calling attention to the effects of being on a side on those who are on it, to how their shared commitment works back on them to generate new capacities and effects, and to how partisan parts are so much more than their sum.

Some on the left are skeptical of such political belonging. Seeing discipline only as constraint and not as a decision to build collective capacity, they substitute the fantasy that politics can be individual for the actuality of political struggle and movement. This substitution evades the fact that comradeship is a choice—both for the one joining and for the party joined, as I explore below. It also ignores the liberating quality of discipline: When we have comrades, we are freed from the obligation to be and know and do everything on our own; there is a larger collective with a line, program, and set of tasks and goals. We are also freed from our impulses (enjoined by communicative capitalism) to criticize and comment on the outrage of the moment. And we are freed from the cynicism that parades as maturity because of the practical optimism that faithful work engenders. Discipline provides the support that frees us to make mistakes, learn, and grow. When we err—and each of us will—our comrades will be there to catch us, dust us off, and set us right. We aren't abandoned to go it alone.

Disorganized leftists too often remain entranced by the illusion of everyday people spontaneously creating new forms of life that will usher in a glorious future. This illusion fails to acknowledge the deprivations and decapacitations that forty years of neoliberalism have inflicted. If it were true that austerity, debt, the collapse of institutional infrastructures, and capital flight could enable the spontaneous emergence of egalitarian forms of life, we would not see the enormous economic inequalities, intensification of racialized violence, declines in life expectancy, slow death, undrinkable water, contaminated soil, militarized policing and surveillance, and desolate urban and suburban neighborhoods that are now commonplace. Exhaustion of resources includes the exhaustion of human resources. Lots of times people want to do something but they don't know what to do or how to do it. They may be isolated in nonunionized workplaces, overburdened by multiple flextime positions, stretched thin caring for friends and family. Disciplined organization—the discipline of comrades committed to common struggle for an emancipatory egalitarian future—can help here. Sometimes we want and need someone to tell us what to do because we are too tired and overextended to figure it out for ourselves. Sometimes when we are given a task as a comrade, we feel like our small efforts have larger meaning and purpose, maybe even world-historical significance in the age-old fight of the people against oppression. Sometimes just knowing that we have comrades who share our commitments, our joys, and our efforts to learn from defeats makes political work possible where it was not before.

Some leftists agree with everything I've said thus far, yet they add buts. But won't we end up disappointed and betrayed? But won't it all ultimately fail (as it has so many times)? But what about the harms comrades have inflicted on each other in the name of comradeship? But what about the persistence of sexism and racism, bigotry and bias? But what happens when we are no longer on the same side, when we cannot say "we" or acknowledge a side? These questions press consideration of the end of comradeship. Frankly speaking, the critical tendency to reject an idea because of a slew of possible future failures is widespread in left milieus. An intellectual façade masks a failure of political will that would be unconvincing in any other context—don't meet that person for coffee in case you fall in love and later have an expensive and hateful divorce; don't speak at that meeting in case you lose your train of thought and end up sounding stupid; don't take up sport or exercise because you might get injured and you'll never be very good at it anyway; don't live because you will inevitably die. Worries about the end foreclose possibilities of beginning. Yes, relationships end. Failures happen. But failure is nothing to fear— it's something to learn from, a next step. This chapter endeavors to learn from the end of comradeship. It considers four types of ending: expulsion, resignation, drift, and the end of the world. These four types are not always distinct. At times, one blends into the other. Yet they open up the ways that the loss of comradeship has differing causes and effects, results and outcomes. They remind us that the fact of an end should not forestall beginning.

Expulsion

Since at least the Moscow Trials of the 1930s, liberals and social- ists have derided Communist parties for expelling their members. Expulsion seems an indication of dogmatism and intolerance, a failure of democratic inclusion. To be sure, this derision is incon- sistent insofar as some liberals and socialists today criticize Communist parties for sexism and racism (as if there were no internal critique already being waged). The inconsistency stems from the fact that expulsion has been a way that Communists address problems and enforce change. From the perspective of Communists, expulsion is a matter of discipline. A comrade who can no longer be relied on to fight together with us for a common future, who is going instead in their own direction, may need to be expelled. We can't see ourselves as being on the same side because they don't appear to be working for the goals we all share. As Trotsky observed at the Eleventh Party Congress, "It was inadmis- sible . . . for party members to speak about their comrades and leaders in terms of 'We' and 'They', for if they did, they would, whatever their intentions, oppose themselves to the party."[1] Our side fragments, and the sense that the same can be expected of everyone gives way to an awareness that factions are united around their own expectations.

The most infamous expulsions were those of Bolsheviks as the Communist Party of the Soviet Union chewed up and spit out the best of its leaders—Trotsky, Bukharin, Zinoviev, Kamenev, and many others. These expulsions were not completely out of the blue. Already in 1921, the party had purged two hundred thousand of its members.[2] Yet, as Deutscher recounts, the intertwining of continuing expectations of comradeship with the factional power struggles that led to expulsions was unbearably tragic. For example, at one point in their deliberations over a proposal to expel Trotsky, the Central Committee and Central Control Commission demurred:

> Still entangled in shreds of old loyalties, still thinking of their adversaries as comrades, still worried about niceties of party statutes, and anxious to preserve appearances of Bolshevik decorum, they sought once again to come to terms with the Opposition.[3]

Comrades give each other a chance. Prior to their expulsions, most of the Bolsheviks assumed comradeship, an assumption shared even by those who would go on to expel them. As Deutscher writes: "Many Stalinists and Bukharinists were uneasy at the thought of becoming the persecutors and jailers of their own comrades and comrades-in-arms."[4] They got over it. Deutscher recounts the scene as Trotsky was dragged onto the train that would carry him away from Moscow. One of Trotsky's sons called out to the railway workers: "Look, comrades . . . look how they are carrying off comrade Trotsky." The workers stand by, watching—"Not a cry or even a murmur of protest came from them."[5]

Perhaps more illuminating, because less well known and hence less amenable to easy explanation and less easily read as symptomatic of some intrinsic inner defect, is an expulsion that took place in the US Communist Party in 1931. I focus on this example not because it parallels the expulsion of Trotsky but because it doesn't. It thereby gives us a sense of why expulsion might be valuable and necessary and how its benefits extend from comrade, to party, to the people. In 1931, CPUSA conducted a massive trial in Harlem. August Yokinen, a Finnish worker, was tried for racial prejudice, upholding white superiority, and forwarding views detrimental to the working class. Some 1,500 black and white workers attended the trial, which was held in the Harlem Casino, one of the biggest halls in the area.[6] A jury of fourteen workers, seven black and seven white, delivered the verdict.

The events leading up to Yokinen's trial unfolded at a Finnish club in Harlem. One evening, three African-American workers showed up for a dance the club was hosting. They were reluctantly admitted, but the hostility of some of the white workers was such that the black workers soon felt they had leave. Yokinen was one of several party members at the dance, none of whom defended the black workers, meaning that none fulfilled "their responsibilities and duties as Party members."[7] The white party members neglected to take "a decisive stand for the defense of the right of the Negro workers to attend this dance together with the white workers."[8] They failed to put equal rights in practice. Instead, they tried to smooth things over.

The Communist Party Committee of the Harlem section investigated the matter, questioning "the comrades in the Finnish club."[9] The Finnish comrades "admitted their mistake . . . *all except Comrade Yokinen*."[10] Yokinen attempted to justify his behavior by saying that he was worried that the black workers would go into the pool room, a room for bathing, "and that he for one, did not wish to bathe with Negroes."[11]

At Yokinen's trial, Clarence Hathaway, the editor of the *Daily Worker*, presented the case for prosecution. Richard B. Moore, "the Party's greatest black orator," carried the defense.[12] Each of their speeches detailed for the audience the Communist Party's position that the struggle for black freedom and racial equality was central to working class struggle. Each emphasized the party's commitment to eliminating white chauvinism from its ranks. Each agreed that Yokinen was guilty. The defense produced a statement from him (translated from Finnish; Yokinen was not fluent in English) that admitted guilt and promised to rectify it through concrete work toward eliminating race prejudice and supporting the black liberation struggle. The disagreement between the prosecution and the defense was over the penalty: should Yokinen be expelled from the Communist Party or put on probation?

Hathaway's case for expulsion focused on how Yokinen was guilty of views and practices that hindered class unity and violated fundamental laws of the Communist Party. Yokinen hindered class unity in several ways. First, the prosecutor claimed that the accused repeated the "white-superiority lies that have been developed consciously by the capitalists and the Southern slave-owners."[13] Hathaway was acknowledging that Yokinen hadn't come up with his prejudicial views on his own but repeated ideas he got from others. These ideas were "systematically and persistently implanted among the workers of this country by the capitalists." Yokinen thus operated as a "phonograph for the capitalists."[14] Hathaway explained to the jury and audience that capitalists promoted white superiority in order to justify the "brutal exploitation and the vicious persecution of the Negro masses by the capitalists in the United States."[15] Therefore even the slightest expression of race superiority turned white workers into "the agents of the bourgeoisie inside the working class movement."[16] By transmitting racist views instead of acting according to the egalitarian expectations of the Communist Party, Yokinen undermined party efforts to build unity among black and white workers.

Hathaway's second argument was that Yokinen indirectly supported the double oppression of black workers. Hathaway reminded those present at the trial that the ideology of white superiority and race hatred was the foundation for lynching and Jim Crow. He told the assembled workers:

Comrade Yokinen, of course, is against all this. He is against lynching and persecution. But unconsciously, Comrade Yokinen with his theories weakens all the efforts to bring about the unity between the white and Negro workers in common struggle against the ruthless and bloody exploiters.[17]

To bring home the seriousness of Yokinen's crime, Hathaway noted that forty-three "Negro workers and poor farmers were lynched last year."[18] He linked these crimes to black courage and militancy, saying that Southern whites typically presented lynching as a response to the charge of rape but that this was a lie. Hathaway explained:

When you go to the root of these "rape" cases, we find not rape but that the Negro is lynched because he refuses to accept the accounting that he is given by the landlord's store. They refuse to be enslaved by the landowners, and it is principally for these reasons that 43 lynchings took place last year.[19]

In the context of lynching and Jim Crow, Yokinen's failure to welcome and support black workers in practice put him on the side of the lynchers and landlords. Instead of advancing the courageous struggle of black workers and farmers, the defendant's actions hindered it. His white chauvinism made the development of class unity impossible, thereby strengthening "the enemies of the workers—capitalists and landlords."[20] The position of the Communist Party, though, was that white supremacy had to be "categorically condemned as anti-working class."[21] Yokinen failed to uphold this position; hence, he must be expelled.

Hathaway's third argument was that Yokinen, whom he referred to throughout the trial as "Comrade Yokinen," violated the views of the party. The prosecution repeatedly asserted the Communist Party's commitment to "complete and unconditional equality for the Negroes."[22] This meant the abolition of laws and practices, laws discriminating against black people in employment, housing, and voting; laws prohibiting interracial marriage; and the broader array of social practices—like dancing and bathing at the Finnish Club— that inscribed racial hierarchy. Mark Naison emphasizes the "landmark" quality of the party's approach to race relations: "Never before had a political movement, socialist or otherwise, tried to create an interracial community that extended into [the] personal sphere, and defined participation in this community as a political duty."[23] Comradeship had to impact everyday life. To draw out how committed the Communist Party was to complete and uncondi- tional racial equality, Hathaway told the story of Comrade Dunne, a party organizer who had recently given a speech in the South. The organizer was asked whether he would ever want his sister "to marry a n----r." Comrade Dunne replied that "he would sooner have his sister marry a militant, fighting Negro, determined to secure equality, than any yellow-bellied white chauvinist."[24] The audience applauded. When Yokinen failed to uphold the party's commitment to racial equality in action, Hathaway observed, he gave black workers good reason to expect nothing but betrayal.

As a contrast to Yokinen's actions, Hathaway explained the Communist Party's commitment to black people's self-determination in the Black Belt (discussed in chapter two). He made clear to the audience of black and white workers the difference between the Communist Party line and the Garveyite position that African Americans should return to Africa:

> We say that the Negro masses have helped to build this country, to establish its institutions and to create its wealth. These Negro masses today are just as much American as any one of us here. They have a right to live in this country on terms of complete freedom.[25]

Because African Americans worked the fields that created the wealth of the US South, that land rightly belonged to them. Thus, the Communist Party was fighting to take that land away from the Southern landowners and give it to the sharecroppers and tenant farmers.

Hathaway concluded by reiterating that it was the duty of white workers to defeat lynching and "unhesitatingly jump at the throat of any person who strikes a Negro in the face, who persecutes a Negro."[26] Because the struggle for the equal rights of black people was so crucial to the proletarian struggle, the Communist Party had to prove in action that it was committed to wiping out every trace of white chauvinism. It had to demonstrate its commitment by expelling Yokinen from the party. Nevertheless, Hathaway offered Yokinen a path back to the party. If Yokinen fought actively against white supremacy, selling the black newspaper *The Liberator* and reporting on his trial at the Finnish Workers Club, then he should be able to apply for readmission.

Moore's defense focused on working-class justice: the principle that should decide Yokinen's punishment entailed insuring "the development of the struggle of the working class and the unity of all the oppressed toilers."[27] Reminding the jury that Yokinen had come to admit his guilt, Moore announced: "But it is not Comrade Yokinen alone who is on trial here. No, fellow-workers, the vicious *capitalist system* which exploits all the workers, this vile, corrupt, oppressive system is the chief criminal in this working class trial."[28] The landlords and bourgeoisie are the ones who spread the poison of race hatred—aided by union and socialist opportunists. Moore's point was not that Yokinen should not be held accountable. It was that no one was innocent. Every aspect of capitalist imperialism spreads the corrupt ideology of white superiority. Moore even turned his critique back on the Communist Party, asking whether it had done the requisite educational work to confront race hatred. Had it developed programs for the workers' movement explaining the importance of the struggle against lynching? Had it made a serious effort to root out prejudice? Moore declared that the answer was no. The party shared in Yokinen's crime. Expelling

Comrade Yokinen would not remove the "taint of chauvinism" from the party or liberate the party from its prejudice.[29] Moore thus concluded that self-criticism, not expulsion, was the better way. Self-criticism would enable the party to prove its commitment through its deeds and "actually work and fight side by side with the doubly oppressed Negro masses, against the bosses' Jim-Crow lynch system, for full equality and self-determination."[30] An added benefit, Moore argued, was that self-criticism would save Yokinen for the struggle, a crucial factor when every worker needed to be brought in to the effort to bring the system down.

Moore emphasized the seriousness of expulsion:

> We must remember that a verdict of expulsion in disgrace from the Communist Party is considered by a class-conscious worker as worse than death at the hands of the bourgeois oppressors. As for myself, I would rather have my head severed from my body by the capitalist lynchers than to be expelled from the Communist International.[31]

Being cut off from the party, separated from one's comrades and deprived of their comradeship, is a fate worse than death. It is the kind of social death where a worker becomes an outsider to his own movement, a person as bad as or worse than the capitalists themselves. Moore painted a vivid picture of the global struggle of the working class against imperialism. He linked the "terror and suffering and misery of the Negro workers" to that of Russian workers and peasants, to oppressed workers in Finland, to the Chinese workers butchered by the Kuomintang, to colonized workers in India, and to all the masses oppressed by the British social-fascist imperialist government in Africa and other colonies. Were Comrade Yokinen to be expelled, he would be lost, world-less, alone.

Moore concluded that Yokinen should be condemned, but argued that "we must first and foremost condemn the bloody, brutal, vicious system of capitalism which breeds unemployment and wage cuts, which breeds starvation and misery, which breeds lynching and terror, which breeds racial and nationalist preju- dice."[32] The party should save and educate its comrade, putting him on probation and giving him a chance to prove that he could fight "for the unity of the working class."[33] It should also engage in ruthless struggle against white chauvinism and anything else that threatened class unity.

The jury found Yokinen guilty, which was not surprising since he had already admitted his guilt. They agreed to expel him but were split on whether the expulsion should last for six or twelve months. They accepted the prosecution's suggestions for the ways Yokinen could correct his mistakes: by reporting on his trial at the Finnish Club, by fighting to have the club admit black workers, by "actively participat[ing] in the struggle against white chauvinism throughout Harlem," by joining the League of Struggle for Negro rights and selling *The Liberator*, and by taking a leading role in the struggle against white chauvinism in every organization to which he belonged.[34] Even though Yokinen was expelled, he remained a comrade. The trial resulted in a decision that affirmed his role in the class struggle, a role focused on eliminating white chauvinism. The party didn't cut him off. They provided him with a path back.

The day after the trial, Yokinen was arrested and held for depor- tation.[35] The *Daily Worker* explained that the bourgeoisie had expected him to become a rat after being expelled from the party. Instead, Yokinen committed himself to fighting for race equality and working-class solidarity. Imploring readers to defend Comrade Yokinen, the newspaper declared:

> Just as the Negroes are lynched and burned at the stake here, so the revolutionary workers are murdered there. And Comrade Yokinen, who Sunday prepared himself to take up the fight against the lynchers here, is to be sent to the Finnish butchers there.[36]

In retrospect, it could seem like the *Daily Worker* was indulging in rhetorical flourish for the sake of furthering the party line on the centrality of the struggle against white supremacy to the proletarian struggle. A year and half after the initial arrest, however, the paper quoted the US Court of Appeals, which had upheld the deportation order. Noting Yokinen's expulsion, the court argued that "it is enough that the alien Yokinen pledged himself to perform certain tasks prescribed by the Communist Party to secure reinstatement. On this ground the relator is deportable."[37] This confirms that Yokinen was in fact being deported because of his agreement to follow the Communist Party line and devote himself to the struggle for black liberation. The paper quoted Yokinen: "A Communist must be true to his Party and carry out its principles not only in words but in deeds. I have carried out these principles. I would rather be deported than be false to them and lose the trust of my comrades."[38]

The story of August Yokinen is not exactly a story of the end of comradeship. Even though he was expelled from the party, the party did not deprive him of comradeship. On the contrary, the Comintern-backed International Labor Defense (ILD) defended him during his deportation hearings. Yokinen was expelled, but not forever banished. Expulsion was an end but it wasn't complete or final; it was a moment. This gives us a view of the end of comradeship that Harry Haywood associates with rectification.[39] Comrades will make mistakes, mistakes that will violate party principles and damage the proletarian struggle, mistakes that must be condemned. But that does not have to mean that they must be cut off forever. Workers' justice and communist principle require that comrades be given a chance to return.

Haywood treats the Yokinen trial as correct practice. By the early 1950s, CPUSA practices had degenerated. There was no longer a path back after one's comradeship had ended. Former comrades were shut out completely. Part of the context for this degeneration was the increasing pressure of Cold War anti-communism on the party. In 1948, twelve party leaders were arrested. Their trial began the following year, becoming one of the longest and most widely covered trials in US history. Eleven of the twelve leaders were found guilty (illness prevented the twelfth, William Z. Foster, from being tried). In 1950, the McCarran Internal Security Act, requiring the registration of all Communist organizations was passed. Also known as the Subversive Activities Control Act, the legislation tightened deportation laws and made picketing a federal courthouse into a felony. It further established that the attorney general could create detention centers for people suspected of subversion. The Communist Party reacted by dissolving branches and sending members underground, moves that Haywood considers hysterical and liquidationist.[40] At the same time, police and FBI infiltration made party work increasingly difficult: provocateurs tried to incite violent and illegal actions, thereby putting party members at risk, undermining trust, and fraying comradeship.

The party was also moving to the right. The rightward shift had started earlier under the leadership of Earl Browder. As Haywood explains, Browder emphasized American national unity. Capital and labor, as he saw it, could work hand in hand for full employment, prosperity, and economic growth. As part of this overall deradicalization of US communism, Browder abandoned the emphasis on African Americans' right of self-determination (he was challenged by Claudia Jones in an article that set off an intense party-wide debate).[41] Browder believed that "Blacks had already achieved full equality" and "had already exercised the historic right of self-determination and opted for integration into the country as a whole."[42] Although Browder was ultimately expelled, the emphasis on coalition work, progressive alliance, and reformism continued.

This was the context for what Haywood describes as the party's "phony war" against white chauvinism.[43] The party's abandonment of its prior commitment to African-American self-determination, along with its general move to the right, created a situation where racist attitudes and practices could again be expressed. According to Haywood, the party should have responded with a new education campaign, mass work, and a "reaffirmation of our revolutionary line."[44] Instead, "a kind of moral crusade was launched which was completely divorced from mass work."[45] Haywood writes:

> Refusing to examine the full implications of Black oppression as national oppression, it was assumed that chauvinist practices could be eliminated by wiping out the wrong ideas and attitudes of the Party rank and file. White chauvinism came to be considered as a sort of phenomenon; a thing in itself, separate from the fight for Black rights and proletarian revolution.[46]

Involving itself in the popular struggles for black liberation would have trained members how and why to oppose white supremacy. But the party chose to set up investigations and hearings, to censure and expel even long-term members. Instead of engaging in the kind of popular organizing that had garnered it the support and respect of many African Americans, the party started to measure its commitment to black liberation by "the number of comrades against whom disciplinary action was taken."[47]

Haywood reports that the struggle lasted "a good four years," becoming increasingly vicious as black comrades embraced a narrow nationalism that empowered them to treat any disagreement with white comrades as indicative of white chauvinism and as white comrades abdicated responsibility for rallying white workers on behalf of black liberation.[48] White comrades retreated to a position of racist paternalism, viewing all black people, "regardless of their class" as revolutionary.[49] Haywood recalls:

White comrades began to fear visiting Black comrades, afraid they might do or say something that could be considered white chauvinist. The war was even carried to the realm of semantics. Comrades who used expressions like "black coffee" and "black sheep" were liable to be charged with chauvinism.[50]

Haywood's wife, Belle, a white woman, was accused of white chauvinism by a black student at the Jefferson School. The student said that he believed that white women who marry black men "are more chauvinistic than others."[51] The campaign became so intense that virtually the entire Denver branch of the party was liquidated.[52] Far from eliminating racism, the phony war against white chauvinism "created hostility, bitterness and distrust among formerly close comrades."[53]

Not all of Haywood's comrades agreed that the war against racism in the party was phony. The Hollywood screenwriter Paul Jarrico, a Communist Party section head frequently identified as a Communist during the hearings of the House Un-American Activities Committee, thought that one of the few issues about which the party was clearly right was the "fight against white chauvinism." As he said in an interview:

None of us who participated in those fights has anything to be ashamed of, ever. And a lot to be proud of. It's all very well to say you're against white chauvinism and you're against racism, but we grow up in a society poisoned by racism, and how do you get rid of that poison?[54]

Expulsions are a way that comradeship ends. It's easy to see this in the case of the expelled individual. Haywood's recollection of a time when expulsions ran amok, when the party entered into a self-destructive frenzy, lets us see the broader impact of expulsion. Paranoia undermines the trust necessary for comradely criticism and self-criticism. Turning in upon itself, the party turned away from mass struggle; away from the campaigns, organizations, and popular work through which it had actively fought for black liberation. No longer an instrument of struggle, the party disintegrates into a field of struggle. Comrades become combatants, then casualties, cut off from their previous world.

The former comrade is socially dead, disengaged from the activities and relations that had sustained their political life. When he was on trial, Bukharin described the position of the expelled as "isolated from everybody, an enemy of the people, in an inhuman position, completely isolated from everything that constitutes the essence of life."[55] It doesn't matter if the comrade was right, if they had integrity or good reasons for what they did. Out on their own, they are not with the party. Their work and actions are not aligned with the larger struggle. For Jessica Mitford, expulsion was akin to being "cast into the outer darkness, the weeping and gnashing of teeth." The hellishness of expulsion wasn't just about being exiled from politics; it was about losing one's entire social being. Mitford writes:

> Once expelled, the former member was "put on nonassociation," meaning that at one blow he or she was severed forever not only from the organization and all its activities, but from a whole circle of long-time friends and acquaintances. To continue to see a person on nonassociation was itself one of the most serious breaches of discipline, and cause for expulsion.[56]

Speaking from the position of the party, former CPUSA member Sophie Chessler explains:

> It wasn't that we didn't feel badly when someone was expelled. We *did*. Very badly. But Party discipline had at all costs to be upheld, defended. This was a fundamental no one questioned. And when someone was expelled it was because—and this we could always see *clearly*—Party discipline was being threatened.[57]

But, as we learn from the Yokinen trial, other paths are available. Comrades can be given another chance. When the superegoic dimension of discipline takes over, such options are lost. The collective desire for collectivity shifts into a drive for impossible purity, as if that purity could install the element needed for the party to endure in a harsh and changing context. Promising relief from the problems facing the party, expulsion instead serves as an impediment to grappling with the problems critically and straightforwardly. Fear makes self-criticism impossible. It's almost as if the McCarthyism threatening the party with arrests and deportations from without manifested within the party as inquisition and expulsion. But just almost: white chauvinism was real, indicated not simply by the attitudes of the rank and file but by the change in the line on black self-determination.

Resignation

Whereas expulsion is a way that the party declares an end to comradeship, resignation occurs when the comrade realizes they are no longer on the same side as their group or party. In the winter of 1962, C. L. R. James resigned from *Correspondence*, a workers' newspaper that he founded a decade earlier. The editor of *Correspondence*, Grace Lee, and chair, James Boggs, had declined to publish a couple of articles James had written that discussed a book by Raymond Williams. The publishing question turned on whether the articles were matters of internal deliberation over the line and direction of the organization or were of broader interest. James brought the question to the larger group of *Correspondence* editing committees. The majority supported publishing the articles. But Lee and Boggs refused to publish them and split the organization.

The political issues underlying the split had been brewing for some time. They involved the paper's position on unions, elites, Marxism, the character of struggles in the United States, and "the revolutionary capacity of the working class."[58] My interest here is less in the details of the dispute than in how the comrade appears in James's response. In the first of three passages from his statement to the editorial board, James presents a commitment to Marxist principles as the basis for comradeship:

> Those who declare that the very fundamentals of Marxism are matters for discussion are no longer Marxists. I am unable to maintain any association whatever with people claiming to be Marxists and conducting themselves in that way. My experience has been that those who seek new and quick roads out of Marxism, while unwilling to declare their break with it, usually become the bitterest and most unscrupulous enemies of former comrades.[59]

In the second passage, James explains his resignation:

> The same motives which prompted me to found the organization and remain devoted to it for twenty years now compel me to sever all connection with those who subscribe to that resolution which expresses the destruction of all we have stood for. I remain as I have always been, the unremitting enemy of all those who, calling themselves Marxists, believe that the building of socialism by the proletariat is a matter for discussion.[60]

And, in the third passage, James addresses his friends, comrades, and enemies:

> With all those who still accept the foundations of Marxism and of our movement I continue to be not only a comrade (which, with all that it implies, counts first with me), hoping that nothing will ever make me depart from that comradely collaboration and personal sympathy with which I have always associated the practice of Marxism . . . the world around us is

in social and spiritual torment precisely because of the abandonment of the idea that the proletariat is the only part of society which can give the impetus to the reorganization of society . . . To all who adhere to that cause, we are comrades, missing no opportunity to advance it. To those who do not know this but are drawn towards resistance to capitalism, we are friends. But to those who, having for years accepted it, are now determined to depart from it, we are enemies, outspoken and relentless.[61]

Each passage mentions comrades and enemies. Comrades are those on the same side, a side James defines by adherence to Marxism. Someone who questions the fundamentals of Marxism is not a comrade because they don't accept the basic commitments that constitute being on the same side.

In the first passage, James rejects those who call themselves Marxists but nevertheless want to debate fundamental tenets of Marxism. In the second passage, he tells us what specific tenet he holds to be inviolable, a litmus test for comrades: the view that socialism is built by the proletariat. In the third, he reiterates his conviction that it is only the proletariat that can spur the socialist reorganization of society. He cannot be comrades with anyone who rejects this idea.

James also identifies the enemy—not the bourgeoisie, not the capitalists, not the bosses and landlords. Enemies call themselves Marxists while questioning its tenets. They are enemies because they destroy the side from within, unraveling the very meaning of Marxism, the very sense of the side. James resigned from *Correspondence* rather than accept this unraveling.

Perhaps because of his passionate sense that former comrades are the bitterest and most unscrupulous enemies, James understands friends differently from the way I present them in chapter three. For James, friends are those who share the political intuition that capitalism is to be resisted. Friends are more than allies interested in transactions that accord with their own self-interest, but less than comrades invested in common Marxist practice. Enemies use the word "Marxist" to describe themselves but don't recognize the proletariat's role in building socialism. Their reference to themselves as "Marxist" feels quixotic, duplicitous, a matter of their own particular definition. To this extent, James's designating former comrades as enemies comes close to my specification of individual identity as the Other of the comrade. A particularistic redefinition of a common term destroys the collectivity produced by being on the same side. When anyone can be a comrade, we need to be sure that we share a politics. Those who claim to speak our language but don't, altering it from within, destroy the very conviction that holds us together. We can't be sure, can't be confident that we are a "we."

Not all resignations are individualistic. Some are righteous assertions of comradeship and collectivity in the context of a party that has lost its way. Junius Scales, who was imprisoned under the Smith Act for membership in the Communist Party, had all sorts of legal and financial problems following his indictment. Scales tells the story of how a loyal party member raised two hundred dollars in her party club to help out him and his family, and the section organizer got wind of what was going on and didn't like it. Scales describes the situation:

> Here was this woman who'd been in the Party for twenty-five years and she's in a room full of people that had been in the Party as long as she had, and this jerk comes in and says that it's against Party policy. She asked why, and he couldn't answer. So she and the whole roomful resigned from the Party on the spot. They went next door and turned over the money they'd raised to my wife.[62]

Comradeship exceeded a claim voiced in the name of the party. The real comrades knew which side they were on.

Many stories where comradeship ends with resignation are vivid, dramatic—membership cards are torn to pieces; former comrades icily address each other as "Citizen," "Mister," or "Miss." Some present the end of comradeship as liberation. In the first of his two memoirs, novelist Howard Fast (author of *Spartacus*) describes his decision to resign from CPUSA as an awakening "from a long and terrible nightmare."[63] His recollections shift between fears of self-extinction, the loss of his individual conscience, acknowledgement of the party's role in his success as a writer, Nikita Khrushchev's 1956 secret speech at the Twentieth Party Congress (which would be the cause of his leaving the party, although Fast didn't announce this for a year), and a longing to leave that had lasted as long as Fast was a member. Fast writes, "The nightmare specified that whosoever left discarded all hope of salvation. That was not easy to live with. Did one begin to leave the Party when one entered it—does one always?"[64] Although Fast testifies to his admiration for rank-and-file cadre, his individualist investment in his career as a writer (even as it was boosted by the party) as well as his testimony to constant ambivalence make one wonder if he was ever a comrade. His second memoir is both less disparaging of the party and more admiring of his own talent and career.[65] Carrying out the expectations of comradeship appears for him to have been a duty rather than a joy, done with reluctance and no small degree of resentment rather than enthusiasm. Nevertheless, he did it.

Other stories of resignation testify to the impact of changes in the party's line; for example, the effects of the party's turn away from the emphasis on black people's right of self-determination. In 1950, Audely "Queen Mother" Moore resigned from CPUSA. Although she said that she had "loved the Party to death," she couldn't go along with its abandonment of a commitment to black people as an oppressed nation. As Moore, who became a well-known black nationalist activist and proponent of reparations for slavery, explained in an interview:

I resigned because I could not get [the party] to discuss the question that was bothering me uppermost on the term "Negro" and the fact that they had relinquished their position as a nation, that we were a nation and I wanted to talk about those things, you know? And when I talked to the whites, they said I made sense. But when I went to the Negro comrades they wouldn't touch it. They had fear, you know, the fear of being politically incorrect, unless the whites had presented it they were afraid and they wouldn't do it so they left me no alternative than to resign you see, because I couldn't go any further the way I was going. I knew I was going wrong, absolutely wrong, detrimental to my own interests as a Negro, yes.[66]

Fear indicates the loss of comradeship. As I emphasize in chapter three, courage is one of the four attributes of the comrade. Unable to get her party to discuss its retreat from its commitment to self-determination for African Americans, Moore could not get it to engage in self-criticism, to admit and address its errors. Members were afraid and thus unable to provide each other with the support, encouragement, and confidence necessary for meaningful party work, for practical optimism. Convinced that the party was no longer a champion of black liberation, Moore left and found other avenues of struggle.[67]

Drift

The end of comradeship is not always dramatic or clear. For some, the intense intimacy of political work slowly dissipates, worn away by exhaustion and disillusionment. Disappointments accrue such that finding one's efforts meaningful and worthwhile becomes harder than doing the work. An organizer for CPUSA describes leaving the party. He didn't resign over a specific cause like after learning about Khrushchev's speech acknowledging the crimes of Stalin era. He stayed on for a number of years. "The world didn't end with a bang it ended with a whimper. The heart was just slowly leaking out of me."[68] The heart leaks out, the sense of intense connection with people on the same side of a struggle diminishes. People realize that their expectations of themselves and each other have changed. Shortly before Frank Wilderson was forced to leave South Africa, his wife said to him: "They're tired of you! They're not *comrades* anymore! They're the government and they're getting tired of you."[69] She was telling him he couldn't expect to be heard, couldn't expect his arguments and appeals to register. The context, the *side*, was gone.

The anticommunist democratic socialist Irving Howe recounts the signs of attenuated attachment to the small socialist sect that had formed around Max Schachtman at the end of the 1940s: "A solid rank-and-filer who for years had collected dues now disappeared without a trace. It's unnerving: he simply stops coming to meetings, a dead soul."[70] Someone expected to show up didn't. That person didn't live up to the expectations comrades have of each other, not even to the extent of explaining why. Howe links the dissolution of the socialist group to the members' efforts to revise or get beyond Marxism. Critical discussion failed to clarify key concepts, resulting instead in fundamental revisions to formerly central ideas and instilling doubts as to the very purpose of the organization. What had been vital became pointless. Howe writes:

> It becomes an ordeal to attend a meeting. You meet people you like yet can hardly bear to look at. Like votaries of a lapsed religion, we go through the routines of "business" and "discussion." We count our losses. We watch from the corners of our eyes to see who is dropping out. We console ourselves with injunctions to "stand fast." We meet less frequently—a help for the nerves. And the more we apply intelligence, the less it conforms to desire.[71]

Diminished involvement led to diminished attachment. Disconnected from common ideas, practices, and struggles, people lost the capacity to see one another as comrades. Worse, they stopped wanting to see the others that way—so why bother?

For Lillian Hellman, the move out of the party was not particularly difficult. She was never all that committed in the first place. Describing herself as "a most casual member," Hellman always prioritized her individual convictions:

> I attended very few meetings and saw and heard nothing more than people sitting around a room talking of current events or discussing the books they had read. I drifted away from the Communist Party because I seemed to be in the wrong place. My own maverick nature was no more suitable to the political left than it has been to the conservative background from which I came.[72]

Like many intellectuals, Hellman valued independence over comradeship. This doesn't make her a bad person. She had been a supporter and fellow traveler, signing "An Open Letter to American Liberals." The letter criticized the efforts made by the American Committee for the Defense of Leon Trotsky to investigate the Moscow Trials, stating that it was necessary to support the Soviet Union as a bulwark against rising fascism in Europe. Hellman also paid for this support; she was blacklisted following her call to appear before the House Un-American Activities Committee. Nevertheless, by her own admission, she was not absorbed in the intense political engagement that connected comrades with each other while separating them from everybody else. Drift came easily.

Use of "comrade" as a term of address isn't enough to combat drift. Compelling people to use the term may actually indicate the loss or absence of comradeship, the fact that people don't expect others to respond as comrades. At various times, the Communist Party of China has instructed cadre to address each other as "*Tongzhi.*" A recent directive told members not to call each other "boss," "buddy," or "bro" because these terms "are known to be used in private enterprises, or even mafia circles."[73] The Communist Party's insistence on the use of the term comrade cuts through economic hierarchies; the equality of political work is not to be confused with the inequalities associated with work done in and for the market. But commanding use of the term undercuts the enthusiasm, joy, and courage associated with the comrade. In this context, actions don't stem from discipline; they stem from fear of the repercussions of not following orders. Moshe Levin writes:

> The use of the term "comrade" loses its magic if the "comrade" is a superior who issues orders and determines your salary and promotion prospects. The new reality, which is now part of daily life, is very simple: "We are not on an equal footing but on a ladder, comrade Ivanov, and I am not your comrade, comrade Ivanov."[74]

There is not one end of comradeship. There are many. After splitting off from one formation, some comrades go on to start new ones—we might think here of Rosa Luxemburg and Karl Liebknecht, who resigned from the German Social Democratic Party and started the Communist Party of Germany. When Jay Lovestone and his comrades were expelled from CPUSA, they insisted they were still Communists and named their new association the Communist Party (Opposition). Although Sylvia Pankhurst announced, "I am tired, comrades. I have had a long and hard struggle" upon being expelled from the Communist Party of Great Britain, she began putting together a Communist workers' group and then became engaged with antifascist and anticolonial struggles.[75] Other former comrades recant, betray, and inform. Harvey Matusow never found the feeling of belonging, of knowing who he was, of being someone, that led him to join CPUSA.[76] He became an FBI informant, was expelled from the Party, and then fashioned himself into a professional anticommunist witness, one of a number of witnesses who became (in)famous during the McCarthy era. His lover, Elizabeth Bentley, also made a career out of being a renegade, selling herself to the media as a "red spy queen."[77] Some former comrades become sworn enemies. Others find ways to call each other comrade again, although more out of affection for a general sense of shared political concerns than in an acknowledgement of clear commitments. Or maybe the commitment is clear: with respect to former comrades who've become friends or allies, colleagues or coalition partners, one knows not to expect too much.

The End of the World

Doris Lessing's 1962 novel *The Golden Notebook* is the final account of the end of comradeship that I consider. Informed by her experience as a member of the Communist Party of Great Britain, the novel depicts the decline and exodus that spread throughout the communist world in the wake of Khrushchev's revelations regarding the purges, arrests, imprisonments, and executions occurring under Stalin. Lessing sets a scene of exhaustion, cynicism, hopelessness, and disarray: The best I can hope for when you are not my comrade, when there are no comrades, is a tired-old liberalism. And given the psychosis that sets in with the collapse of the party, even this small dream feels impossible. In ways that echo James's resignation from *Correspondence*, Lessing presents the end of comradeship as the unraveling of a common language, of the shared sense of the meaning of words and their relation to the world. She takes the idea further, presenting the dissolution of confidence in the party as psychosis. In contrast to drift, in which a symbolic communist world continues even if one is not part of it, Lessing gives us a picture in which the symbolic order has collapsed, a picture of the end of the world.

The Golden Notebook is structured around a short novel appearing in five installments, *Free Women*, and four sets of notebooks labelled by color—black, red, yellow, and blue. One of the main characters in *Free Women*, Anna Wulf, keeps these notebooks as a way to order her thoughts: "She has to separate things off from each other, out of fear of chaos, of formlessness—of breakdown."[78] Warding off chaos is the condition Anna finds herself in at the beginning of the 1950s, as cynicism in the party increases and her attachment to the party declines. Anna produces a final notebook, the golden one, after the fourth installment of *Free Women* and four rounds of entries in the original notebooks. The golden notebook attempts to bring together the fragmented themes of the other four, to integrate what had been fragmented and separate. This integration also depicts Anna's psychotic break, as well as the end of a relationship and step back toward writing.

Free Women begins in 1957 with a conversation that takes place in a London apartment between Anna, the author of one successful novel, and her friend Molly, a minor actress who has recently returned from a year's travel in Europe. Molly's ex-husband, Richard, arrives at the apartment to cajole her about their twenty-year old son, Tommy. Richard is bothered by the fact that Tommy is suffering from "a paralysis of the will."[79] Tommy won't accept any of the business opportunities his father has tried to open up for him, nor will he "go to Oxford, and now he sits around, brooding."[80] Richard attributes Tommy's malaise to the collapse of the Communist Party, saying to the two women:

> It hasn't occurred to you that the real trouble with Tommy is that he's been surrounded half his life with communists or so-called communists—most of the people he's known have been mixed up in one way and another. And now they're all leaving the party, or have left—don't you think it might have had some effect?[81]

Anna and Molly agree; of course this has occurred to them. The impact of events taking place in the world in the last year—Khrushchev's speech, the invasion of Hungary, the Suez Crisis—has been severe. "It's not an easy time to be a socialist."[82] Richard pushes the point: "And now what? Russia's in the doghouse and what price the comrades now? Most of them having nervous breakdowns or making a lot of money, as far as I can make out."[83] Collapse and capitalism—this captures the sense of many of those who left the party in the wake of Khrushchev's revelations, the non-options available to them in a world thrown into chaos. Collapse and capitalism: our present of anxiety, depression, and despair in the extremes of climate change, inequality, and the worry that we may no longer be able to afford to live. Collapse and capitalism: our setting of survivors and systems.

The principles that had previously guided party work, the discipline that insured cadre that they knew what they could expect from their comrades, were now objects of disgust or, for Molly, boredom. As she explains, Molly is done with communist politics:

> Two or three years ago I felt guilty if I didn't spend all my free time organizing something or other. Now I don't feel at all guilty if I simply do my job and laze around for the rest. I don't care anymore, Anna. I simply don't.[84]

Molly has already distanced herself from the party and her former comrades. Previously, she was always "rushing off to organize something, full of life and enthusiasm."[85] Now she feels no obligation to continue doing political work. Anna still feels something, a continued tie or connection to those she thinks of as comrades. Yet she is exhausted, confused, and uncertain, wrapped up in trying to understand the loss of a "great dream."[86]

The red notebook contains Anna's thoughts about the Communist Party of Great Britain. The first entry is dated January 3, 1950, a day or so before Anna joins the party, "the first intellectual prepared to join the Party since the cold war started."[87]

Molly was already a member and Anna is attracted to "the atmosphere of friendliness, of people working for a common end."[88] Yet Anna doesn't consider herself a joiner. She is also hesitant about becoming a member of an organization that she suspects to be dishonest. Nevertheless, she joins, in part because of two feelings she has upon seeing the protective glass shielding the offices at the party headquarters: "one of fear; the world of violence. The other, a feeling of protectiveness—the need to protect an organization that people throw stones at."[89] The feeling of fear makes Anna think about why people join the Communist Party of Great Britain: It's hard for people in England "to remember the realities of power, of violence; the C.P. represents to them the realities of naked power that are cloaked in England itself."[90] The struggle is real—even in England. The feeling of protectiveness inspires in Anna a desire to defend the Soviet Union from the attacks she reads about in the papers and hears from non-Communist associates. Anna doesn't make many entries in the red notebook over the next few years. She observes that most of her remarks on the party are critical, yet she and Molly both stay in it.

In the blue notebook that functions most like a diary, Anna's entry recounting a session with her psychotherapist expresses her ambivalence about the party. In response to her therapist's question, "Why are you a communist?" Anna answered, "At least they believe in something." The conversation continued:

> "Why do you say *they*, when you are a member of the Communist Party?" "If I could say *we*, really meaning it, I wouldn't be here, would I?" "So you don't care, really about your comrades?" "I get on easily with everyone, if that's what you mean?" "No, that's not what I mean."

Anna told her therapist that she swings between fearing and hating the party and desperately clinging to it "out of a need to protect it and look after it."[91] What pushes her away from the party attaches her to it. Before returning to personal recollections, the blue notebook shifts to newspaper clippings that document several years of international tension and horror: the war in Korea, the detonation of the H-bomb, the anticommunist witch hunt in the United States, the purges in the Soviet bloc, and so on. The Communist Party is awful and yet it seems that it is the only barrier to US nuclear aggression. Britain explodes an atomic weapon. The McCarran Act authorizes the US attorney general to create detention centers for people who might engage in conspiracy or espionage. The Mau Mau uprising contests British colonial rule in Kenya. Communist leaders are hanged in Prague. Defending the Soviet Union at all costs, the party doesn't provide a space for grappling with the truth of the world, yet without the party, the world feels bereft, meaningless, condemned to a façade of liberalism that masks imperialism, authoritarianism, and colonialism.

In the second installment of *Free Women*, Tommy confronts Anna about her and his mother, Molly, abandoning all the activity that had so occupied them for years as members of the Communist Party. Anna demurs by pointing out that middle-aged women can't be expected to hold on to "youthful certainties and slogans and battle-cries."[92] But she dislikes what she hears coming out of her mouth: "I sound like a tired old liberal."[93] Tommy observes that Anna "used to live by a philosophy," taunts her for referring to "the communist myth," and demands to know what she lives by now.[94] Anna's reply is positive, hopeful. She describes a world capable of forward movement, a dream kept alive for a new generation of people. Tommy makes it clear that he won't be that generation. He shoots himself. The second installment ends with the likelihood that Tommy will die before morning.

The red notebook starts up again in August 1954 with Anna telling her lover, Michael, that she is thinking of leaving the party. Michael replies that Anna speaks as if the effect of her leaving the party would be that she would end up in some kind of "morass of moral turpitude." He finds this absurd given "the fact that literally millions of perfectly sound human beings have left the Party (if they weren't murdered first) and they left it because they were leaving behind murder, cynicism, horror, betrayal."[95] The fact of their leaving doesn't address the impact that the party's disintegration had on its members, the way that the dissolution of its structure of meaning marked the end of the world. Nevertheless, it does open up the inner decay of language symptomatic of the party's unraveling. In the face of murder, cynicism, horror, and betrayal, what does it mean to be a comrade? Does it mean dissemblance and hypocrisy, committed defense of practices one feels are wrong in the name of a goal one is convinced is right?

A subsequent entry in the red notebook goes back in time, to a writers' group meeting in 1952. The regress belies the hopeful linearity of Anna's response to Tommy: Life had not gotten better, Comrade. The entry concerns itself with changes in language, conflicting modalities of meaning and tone. The writers' group is unsuccessfully trying to discuss an unreadable pamphlet by Stalin on linguistics. Anna observes a tone in the group's discussion that makes her uncomfortable, a tone associated with making excuses, "of course you have to remember their legal traditions are very different from ours."[96] She recalls that she caught herself speaking this way and "started to stammer. I usually don't stammer."[97] Anna also notes an increasingly familiar mood:

> Words lose their meaning suddenly. I find myself listening to a
> sentence, a phrase, a group of words, as if they are in a foreign
> language—the gap between what they are supposed to mean,
> and what in fact they say seems unbridgeable.[98]

Comrades fail to say what they all know to be true: Stalin's pamphlet is a symptom of "a general uneasiness about language."[99] But as comrades they can no longer speak together. They are caught in a situation where the words they are able to say are inadequate

to what needs to be said. Anna observes that she's prepared to
believe that Stalin "is mad and a murderer"; nevertheless, she likes

> to hear people use that tone of simple, friendly respect for him.
> Because if that tone were to be thrown aside, something very
> important would go with it, paradoxically enough, a faith in
> the possibilities of democracy, of decency. A dream would be
> dead—for our time, at least.[100]

The tone of respect points to comradeship, to being on the same
side. It's not the same as the tone of excuses. Using the tone of
respect when speaking of Stalin isn't a sign that one is a Stalinist—
that is to say, it doesn't indicate that one makes excuses for
purges and camps. It rather indicates belief in collective struggle
for a better world. And the thing is this, something that even
anti-Stalinist skeptics have to admit is right: the end of the twentieth-
century socialist experiment destroyed democracy. The tone of
respect was thrown aside. A dream of emancipated equality died.

As the entries in the blue notebook continue into September
1954, Anna describes her decision to leave the party. She knows she
will miss being in an atmosphere where people take it "for granted
that their lives must be related to a central philosophy."[101] She
regrets the upcoming separation from her friend, colleague, and
comrade Jack, a "good communist."[102] Soon, when they meet, they
will be strangers.[103] Yet she can no longer bear what she sees as the
"steadily debasing values of the Party" or the "intellectual rotten-
ness" that leads it to publish shoddy books that reflect the lies that
it tells itself.[104] Anna is tired of the myth that the Communist Party
of Great Britain continues to believe about what it is and does. She
is exhausted by the overabundance of dead writing she confronts as
a manuscript reader for the party publishing house. She finds this
writing banal and impersonal, while she herself has come to believe
that real art comes from "genuine personal feeling."[105] This belief
has ruptured her capacity to do her party work, which is lecturing

on art. Her typical lecture involves a critique of the egotism of bourgeois art. In the middle of a lecture she gives several months before leaving the party, she again "began to stammer and couldn't finish." Anna continues: "I have not given any more lectures. I know what that stammer means."[106] Jack agrees that most communist art is bad. But he thinks communal art needs time—not individual sensibility. Jack tells Anna, "There's something very arrogant about insisting on the right to be right."[107] But Anna already feels the separation between them. Her decision to leave the party is an effect, not a cause, of the dissolution of the connection between words and meaning. Even in her conversation with Jack, she experiences this loss—"words lose their meaning"; she can hear their voices, but the words "don't mean anything."[108] In the place of words, she sees images—"scenes of death, torture, cross-examination and so on"—that connect not to the words being used but to the reality they disavow.

The third installment of *Free Women* reveals that Tommy's suicide attempt failed. He lives—now blind, a dominating "all-conscious presence" in Molly's house. Molly is trapped, both by him and by a new sense that life has become a matter of "getting used to things that are really intolerable."[109] Although Tommy is slow and careful since his loss of vision, "like some kind of zombie," he seems happy. Molly describes him as "all in one piece for the first time in his life"—yet she is horrified by her own words, "matching them against the truth of that mutilation."[110] The truth is that "he enjoys it."[111] Tommy no longer has to choose; he no longer has to feel compelled to find a way forward. He can be where he is, fully occupying that place without having to analyze, understand, or see it. It's as if blindness gives Tommy the capacity to force a maternal scene onto Molly, to envelope her into an infantile oneness that makes him complete at the cost of her misery. In Lacanian jargon, Tommy's loss of vision suggests the loss of the symbolic and the formlessness that comes with the merging of the imaginary and the Real. Molly and Tommy don't remain intertwined. He attaches to his stepmother and then to a wife, and drifts into an incoherent, formless politics of spontaneous crowds and expressive students.

Anna's corresponding blue notebooks continue the theme of formlessness. She feels herself breaking down: "Words mean nothing," existing more and more as just "a series of meaningless sounds, like nursery talk."[112] When Anna writes words down, they dissolve into images that have nothing to do with them. She's afraid. She stops dating her entries, as if the calendar itself has come to lack an organizing capacity. Anna starts to fall in love with Saul Green, an American socialist boarding in her house who is himself breaking down. In conversation with Anna, Saul talks compulsively, saying nothing. Anna writes, "I was listening for the word *I* in what he said. I, I, I, I, I—I began to feel as if the word I was being shot at me like bullets from a machine gun."[113] This compulsive talking, this I, I, I, I, I becomes a mark of Saul's madness. The talking sometimes carries streams of political jargon that Anna can identify by time and tendency: "Trotskyist, American, early 19-fifties. Premature anti-Stalinist, 1954."[114] Anna herself becomes sicker and sicker, obsessed with Saul and spending more time sleeping and dreaming. They begin to call each other comrade, using the word "with an ironical nostalgia" born of "disbelief and destruction."[115] Saul observes: "As I crack up out of that 100 per cent revolutionary, I notice I crack up into aspects of everything I hate."[116] He wants more than anything to return to the happiness of a time when he and others believed that they could change the world. Saul begins again with the compulsive "I, I, I, I like a machine-gun ejaculating regularly."[117] Anna writes: "I was listening and not listening, as if to a speech I had written someone else was delivering. Yes, that was me, that was everyone, the I, I, I, I. I am. I am. I am going to. I won't be. I shall. I want. I."[118] At one point, Saul cries out, "My God, what we've lost, what we've lost, what we've lost, how can we ever get back to it, how can we get back to it again."[119] Then he switches back to the I, I, I, I, as Anna curls up in a sick and drunken ball of pain. The notebook ends with them both moving on as writers, smaller and damaged, but surviving with diminished hope in a system that exceeds their attenuated capacity to understand or change.

The last installment of *Free Women* depicts Anna at the beginning of her relationship with Saul. As her mental health declines, she obsessively clips patches of print from newspapers and pins them to her walls, searching for order every day, a pattern or form to all that is going on. Without the party, without communism to provide meaning and structure, Anna has no idea how to understand the world. In a sort of retroactive prefiguration of the machine-gun effect of Saul's I, I, I, I, Anna experiences herself as "a central point of awareness, being attacked by a million unco-ordinated facts, and the central point would disappear if she proved unable to weigh and balance the facts, take them into account."[120] As we know from the preceding notebook, she won't be able to continue to hold herself together as a central point of awareness. She'll collapse into psychosis and then start to write again.

Tommy finally goes into business with his father, Richard, rationalizing his decision by saying that "the world is going to be changed by the efforts of progressive big business and putting pressure on Government departments."[121] Molly gets remarried. Anna works as a marriage counselor. It's as if Lessing knew Thatcherism was coming: "There's no such thing as society. There are individual men and women and there are families." The loss of the party, of the organizing role of communism in twentieth-century life, is the loss of a perspective that lets society be seen. Tommy, his generation, can't see the world his mother and Anna saw. Former comrades turn to private life as the space and possibility of politics contract to ethics and economics, survivors and systems.

The world that Lessing depicts is the world of the left not just after 1956 but also after 1968 and 1989. It's our world that seems too exhausted even for tired old liberalism. The end of comrade-ship is the end of the world: nonmeaning, incoherence, madness, and the pointless, disorienting insistence on the I.

Sometimes people ask me if we will have comrades after communism arrives. Given the world we inhabit, I find the question either obtusely theoretical or disingenuous—communism seems so far away, is this really your worry? The intuition behind the question is that once the struggle ends, we won't be comrades because there won't be sides. Presumably, at that point, everyone will be a comrade. But what does that mean if anyone but not everyone can be a comrade? The mistake here is in thinking that communism is the end of history rather than history's condition of possibility—the possibility we need if there is to be anything like history in the future. The problems facing the world can only be addressed through communism, as comrades—the class struggle today is the fight for a future. Capitalism is incapable of addressing climate change and the migrations and struggles over resources that will result with anything other than militarism, walls, and genocide. At the same time, comradeship is not risk-free. It is not a magical solution to all problems facing the left, much less the world. But it is the only form through which these problems might be solved. Anything less will doom us to the competition, individualism, cynicism, and melancholia into which we've descended. To be a left at all, we have to be comrades. When I recognize that the question about the existence of comrades after communism comes in fact from a comrade, I can affirm and build on their hope and desire—the question presup-poses that we win. It takes its orientation from communism's victory, continuing to desire the form and relation that makes it possible—the comrade.

Notes

Chapter One: From Allies to Comrades

1. "Here's the Full Transcript of President Obama's Speech at the White House Correspondents' Dinner," *Time*, May 1, 2016, time.com.

2. Juan A. Herrero Brasas, *Walt Whitman's Mystical Ethics of Comradeship*, Albany, NY: SUNY Press, 2010, 86.

3. See the entry for "camarade" in Wiktionary at en.wiktionary.org.

4. I'm indebted to Andre Matlock for this point. See also the entry for "comrade" in Wiktionary at en.wiktionary.org.

5. Angela Y. Davis, *Angela Davis: An Autobiography*, New York: International Publishers, 1988, 187–8.

6. Vivian Gornick, *The Romance of American Communism*, New York: Basic Books, 1978, 110.

7. See Slavoj Žižek, "Class Struggle or Postmodernism?," in *Contingency, Hegemony, Universality: Contemporary Dialogues on the Left*, ed. Judith Butler, Ernesto Laclau, and Slavoj Žižek, London: Verso, 2000, 90–135, at 116–7.

8. Jodi Dean, *Crowds and Party*, London: Verso, 2016, 189.

9. See Jodi Dean, *The Communist Horizon*, London: Verso, 2012; and Dean, *Crowds and Party*.

10. Bernard Aspe, "1917/2017: Revolutions, Communist Legacies and Spectres of the Future," presentation, European University at St. Petersburg, October 24–26, 2017.

11. Astra Taylor, Keith Gessen, and editors from *n+1*, *Dissent*, *Triple Canopy*, and the *New Republic*, eds., *Occupy! Scenes from Occupied America*, London: Verso, 2011.

12. Gornick, *Romance of American Communism*, 202.

13. Frank B. Wilderson III, *Incognegro: A Memoir of Exile and Apartheid*, Durham, NC: Duke University Press, 2015, 275.

14. Ibid., 277.

15. Ibid., 464.

16. Kathi Weeks, *The Problem with Work: Feminism, Marxism, Antiwork Politics, and Postwork Imaginaries*, Durham, NC: Duke University Press, 2011, 204–5.

17. Ibid., 206.

18. Timothy Morton, *Hyperobjects: Philosophy and Ecology after the End of the World*, Minneapolis: University of Minnesota Press, 2013.

19. Wendy Brown, "Wounded Attachments," *Political Theory* 21: 3, August 1993, 390–410. See also Robin D. G. Kelley's critique of black student activists' embrace of the language of personal trauma, in Robin D. G. Kelley, "Black Study, Black Struggle," *Boston Review*, March 7, 2016, bostonreview.net.

20. Jodi Dean, "The Anamorphic Politics of Climate Change," *e-flux* 69, January 2016.

21. Jodi Dean, "Communicative Capitalism: Circulation and the Foreclosure of Politics," *Cultural Politics* 1: 1, 2005, 51–74.

22. Carl Schmitt, *The Concept of the Political*, expanded ed., trans. George Schwab, Chicago: University of Chicago Press, 2007.

23. In addition to Morton, *Hyperobjects*, see Benjamin Bratton,

"Some Trace Effects of the Post-Anthropocene: On Accelerationist Geopolitical Aesthetics," *e-flux* 46, June 2013, e-flux.com.

24. Jennifer M. Silva, *Coming Up Short: Working-Class Adulthood in an Age of Uncertainty*, New York: Oxford University Press, 2013.

25. I have in mind here inquiries focused on extinction, algorithms, post-humanism, and the planetary. See, for example, the contributions to *After Extinction*, Richard Grusin, ed., Minneapolis: University of Minnesota Press, 2018.

26. Jodi Dean, "Faces as Commons: The Secondary Visuality of Communicative Capitalism," Open! Platform for Art, Culture, and the Public Domain, December 31, 2016, onlineopen.org.

27. Not An Alternative, "Institutional Liberation," *e-flux* 77, November 2016, e-flux.com; Jonas Staal, "Assemblism," *e-flux* 80, March 2017, e-flux.com.

28. This may also account for the popularity of the slogan "Nevertheless, she persisted" among US white feminists after Elizabeth Warren was interrupted and chastised for criticizing Alabama senator Jeff Sessions's civil rights record during the Senate hearings for his confirmation as US attorney general. Nevertheless, he was confirmed.

29. "Guide to Allyship," guidetoallyship.com.

30. Another Round, Tracy Clayton, and Heben Nigatu, "How to Be a Better Ally: An Open Letter to White Folks," BuzzFeedNews, December 30, 2015, buzzfeednews.com.

31. Karolina Szczur, "Fundamentals of Effective Allyship," Medium, February 12, 2018, medium.com.

32. Jamie Utt, "So You Call Yourself an Ally: 10 Things All 'Allies' Need to Know," *Everyday Feminism*, November 8, 2013, everydayfeminism.com. Italics in original as boldface.

33. Ibid. Italics in original as boldface.

34. Mark Fisher, "Exiting the Vampire Castle," *openDemocracy*, November 24, 2013, opendemocracy.net.

Chapter Two: The Generic Comrade

1. Angela Y. Davis, *Women, Race and Class*, New York: Vintage Books, 1983, 150.
2. Alexandra Kollontai, "International Socialist Conferences of Women Workers," Marxists Internet Archive, marxists.org.
3. V. I. Lenin, "Theses on the National Question," in *Lenin Collected Works*, vol. 19, Moscow: Progress Publishers, 1977, 243–51.
4. Clara Zetkin, "Lenin on the *Women's Question*," *The Emancipation of Women: From the Writings of V. I. Lenin*, New York: International Publishers, 2011.
5. Ibid.
6. Barbara Foley, *Radical Representations: Politics and Form in U.S. Proletarian Fiction, 1929–1941*, Durham, NC: Duke University Press, 1993, 219.
7. Erik S. McDuffie, *Sojourning for Freedom: Black Women, American Communism, and the Making of Black Left Feminism*, Durham, NC: Duke University Press, 2011, 94.
8. Foley, *Radical Representations*, 219.
9. Murray Kempton, *Part of Our Time: Some Ruins and Monuments of the Thirties*, New York: Simon and Schuster, 1955, 213.
10. Kate Weigand, *Red Feminism: American Communism and the Making of Women's Liberation*, Baltimore: Johns Hopkins University Press, 2001, 23.
11. McDuffie, *Sojourning for Freedom*, 130.
12. Ibid., 112; Louise Thompson Patterson, "Toward a Brighter Dawn (1936)," reprinted in *Viewpoint Magazine*, October 31, 2015, viewpointmag.com.
13. McDuffie, *Sojourning for Freedom*, 171.
14. Margaret Cowl, *Women and Equality*, New York: Workers Library Publishers, 1935.
15. Ibid., 8–10.

16. Ibid., 14.
17. See McDuffie, *Sojourning for Freedom*, 118, and the editors' introduction to Mary Inman, "The Role of the Housewife in Social Production (1940)," *Viewpoint Magazine*, October 2015, viewpointmagazine.com.
18. Weigand, *Red Feminism*, 33.
19. Ibid., 35.
20. Ibid.
21. Ibid., 37.
22. Ibid., 38.
23. Ibid., 39.
24. Ibid., 39.
25. Avram Landy, "Two Questions on the Status of Women under Capitalism," *Communist* XX: 9, September 1941, 818–33, at 822–3.
26. Ibid., 823.
27. Weigand, *Red Feminism*, 43.
28. Ibid., 29.
29. Introduction to Inman, "The Role of the Housewife in Social Production," *Viewpoint*.
30. Landy, "Two Questions on the Status of Women under Capitalism," 821.
31. Weeks, *The Problem with Work*, 203.
32. Robin D. G. Kelley, *Hammer and Hoe: Alabama Communists during the Great Depression*, Chapel Hill: University of North Carolina Press, 1990, 26.
33. See Dayo F. Gore, *Radicalism at the Crossroads: African American Women Activists in the Cold War*, New York: NYU Press, 2011.
34. Davis, *Angela Davis*, 318.
35. Clara Zetkin, "Lenin on the *Women's Question*."
36. See Jacques Lacan, *On Feminine Sexuality: The Limits of Love and Knowledge, Book XX, Encore 1972–1973*, trans. Bruce Fink, New York: Norton, 1999.

37. Zetkin, "Lenin on the *Women's Question*."

38. Ibid.

39. Cedric J. Robinson, *Black Marxism: The Making of a Radical Tradition*, Chapel Hill: University of North Carolina Press, 2000.

40. Biko Agozino, "The Africana Paradigm in *Capital*: The Debts of Karl Marx to People of African Descent," *Review of African Political Economy* 41: 140, 2014, 172–84.

41. Davis, *Women, Race and Class*, 153.

42. Ibid., 154.

43. Mark Solomon, *The Cry Was Unity*, Jackson: University of Mississippi Press, 1998, 6.

44. Ibid., 7.

45. Cyril V. Briggs, "Make Their Cause Your Own," in *Class Struggle and the Color Line: American Socialism and the Race Question 1900–1930*, ed. Paul M. Heideman, Chicago: Haymarket Books, 2018, 240.

46. Robert Whitaker, *On the Lap of the Gods*, New York: Three Rivers, 2009, 47.

47. Ibid., 49.

48. Ibid., 50.

49. Ibid.

50. Ibid.

51. Cyril V. Briggs, "Bolshevism and Race Prejudice," in Heideman, *Class Struggle and the Color Line*, 241.

52. Solomon, *The Cry Was Unity*, 13.

53. Ibid., 16.

54. Wilderson, *Incognegro*, 383.

55. Ibid.

56. See Foley, *Radical Representations*, 170–1.

57. Wilderson, *Incognegro*, 132–3.

58. Mark Naison, "Historical Notes on Blacks and American Communism: The Harlem Experience," *Science & Society* 42: 3, fall 1970, 324–43; the story appears on 324.

59. Claudia Jones, "An End to the Neglect of the Problems of the Negro Woman!," *Words of Fire: An Anthology of African-American Feminist Thought*, ed. Beverly Guy-Sheftal, New York: New Press, 1995, 108–23, at 117.

60. Ibid.

61. Solomon, *The Cry Was Unity*, 21.

62. Ibid., 20.

63. Cyril V. Briggs, "Acid Test of White Friendship," in Heideman, *Class Struggle and the Color Line*, 263–4, at 263.

64. Ibid., 264.

65. Ibid., 263–4.

66. Ibid., 264.

67. Solomon, *The Cry Was Unity*, 135.

68. Mark Naison, *Communists in Harlem during the Depression*, New York: Grove Press, 1983, xv. Nikhil Pal Singh likewise complicates the view that black people are opposed to communism, emphasizing instead the efforts of black intellectuals "to articulate an independent and indigenous black radicalism." Nikhil Pal Singh, *Black Is a Country: Race and the Unfinished Struggle for Democracy*, Cambridge, MA: Harvard University Press, 2004, 122.

69. Lovett Fort-Whiteman, "The Negro in Politics," in Heideman, *Class Struggle and the Color Line*, 334.

70. Robinson criticizes the thesis as opportunist and anchored in an incoherent notion of the nation. Robinson, *Black Marxism*, 226. See also Beverly Tomek, "The Communist International and the Dilemma of the American 'Negro Problem': Limitations of the Black Belt Self-Determination Thesis," *Working USA: The Journal of Labor and Society* 15, December 2012, 549–76.

71. C. L. R. James, in "Self-Determination for the American Negroes," originally published in Leon Trotsky, *On Black Nationalism: Documents on the Negro Struggle* (1939), reissue, Marxists Internet Archive, marxists.org.

72. Harry Haywood, *Black Bolshevik: Autobiography of an Afro-American Communist*, Chicago: Liberator Press, 1978, 157.

73. Ibid., 219.

74. Ibid., 231.

75. Ibid., 231–2.

76. Ibid., 232.

77. Ibid., 229.

78. Ibid., 264.

79. Ibid.

80. Ibid., 234.

81. "Black Belt Thesis," *Daily Worker*, February 12, 1929, 3 reprinted in Heideman, *Class Struggle and the Color Line*, 283–90, at 283.

82. Ibid., 287.

83. Ibid., 286.

84. Solomon, *The Cry Was Unity*, 86.

85. Ibid., 135.

86. "Black Belt Thesis," 288.

87. Solomon, *The Cry Was Unity*, 87.

88. Ibid., 128.

89. Ibid.

90. Ibid., 144–5.

91. Andrei Platonov, *Chevengur*, trans. Anthony Olcott, Ann Arbor, MI: Ardis, 1978. *Chevengur* was not published as a novel in Russian until a partial Russian version appeared in 1972. A more complete Russian version was published in 1988. Fredric Jameson, *The Seeds of Time*, New York: Columbia University Press, 1994, 79.

92. Platonov, *Chevengur*, 243.

93. Isabelle Garo, "Chevengur, the Country of Unreal Communism—The October Revolution through the Dialectical Art of Andréï Platonov," *Crisis and Critique* 4: 2, November 2017, 174–96, at 180.

94. Maria Chehonadskih, "Soviet Epistemologies and the Materialist Ontology of Poor Life: Andrei Platonov, Alexander Bogdanov and Lev Vygotsky," PhD diss., Centre for Research in Modern European Philosophy, Kingston University, 2017, 139.

95. See Artemy Magun, *Negative Revolution*, London: Bloomsbury, 2013.

96. Platonov, *Chevengur*, 231.

97. Ibid., 232.

98. Mao likewise found revolutionary potential in the "poverty and blankness of the Chinese people." As Pang Laikwan explains, "Being 'poor and blank' and deprived of all identity tags, the Maoist subject becomes an empty vehicle ready to be invested with revolutionary will, so that he or she can engage in the most ferocious struggles and bring seemingly impossible historical transformation to fruition." Pang Laikwan, "Dialectical Materialism," in *The Afterlives of Chinese Communism*, eds. Christian Sorace, Ivan Franceschini, and Nicholas Loubere, London: Verso, 2019.

99. Maria Chehonadskih emphasizes that Platonov takes an anticolonial perspective that breaks with the image of a white working class (personal communication with author).

100. This lack of militancy distinguishes Platonov's others from the comrades movement in Natal, South Africa, in the late 1980s. In interviews, young South African militants expressed "a strong sense of 'having nothing'" (634). Yet, even though they had nothing—no job, no education, no food, no way out—they did have a militarized culture of resistance and a sense of social solidarity. Ari Sitas, "The Making of the 'Comrades' Movement in Natal, 1985–1991," *Journal of South African Studies* 18: 3, September 1992, 629–41.

101. R. Chandler, unpublished translation, in Chehonadskih, "Soviet Epistemologies and the Materialist Ontology of Poor Life," 137; cf. Platonov, *Chevengur*, 231.

102. McKenzie Wark, *Molecular Red*, London: Verso, 2015, 106.

103. I am indebted to David Riff for this point.

104. Herbert Bartholmes, *Bruder, Bürger, Freund, Genosse und andere Wörter der sozialistischen Terminologie: wortgeschichtliche Beiträge, Göteborger germanistische Forschungen Acta Universitatis Gothoburgensis* 11, Wuppertal-Barmen, Germany: Hammer Verlag, 1970, 175.

105. Platonov, *Chevengur*, 225.

106. Ibid., 141.

107. Ibid., 228.

108. Ibid., 211.

109. Slavoj Žižek, *Less Than Nothing*, London: Verso, 2013, 967.

110. See Valery Podoroga, "The Eunuch of the Soul," *South Atlantic Quarterly* 90: 2, 1991, 357–407.

111. Platonov, *Chevengur*, 225.

Chapter Three: Four Theses on the Comrade

1. John McCumber, *Time in the Ditch: American Philosophy in the McCarthy Era*, Evanston, IL: Northwestern University Press, 2001, 38–9.

2. Alexandra Kollontai, "New Woman," reprint, trans. Salvator Attansio, in *The Autobiography of a Sexually Emancipated Communist Woman*, Freiburg im Breisgau, Germany: Herder and Herder, (1918) 1971.

3. Alexandra Kollontai, "Communism and the Family," reprint, in *Selected Writings of Alexandra Kollontai*, trans. Alix Holt, London: Allison & Busby, (1920) 1977.

4. I am indebted to Maria Chehonadskih for this example, which comes from G. O. Vinokur, *Kul'tura iazyka*, Moscow, 1929.

5. Alexandra Kollontai, "Sexual Relations and the Class Struggle," reprint, in *Selected Writings of Alexandra Kollontai*.

6. Maxim Gorky, "Comrade," *Social Democrat* X: 8, August 1908, 509–12.

7. See also Brasas, *Walt Whitman's Mystical Ethics of Comradeship* and Kirsten Harris, *Walt Whitman and British Socialism: "The Love of Comrades,"* New York: Routledge, 2016.

8. Amy Wellington, "The Slave of a Slave," *Comrade* 1: 6, 1901, 128.

9. George D. Herron, "A Song of To-Morrow," *Comrade* 3: 4, 1903, 83.

10. George D. Herron, "From Gods to Men," *Comrade* 1: 4, 1901, 97.

11. *Revolution Every Day: A Calendar 1917–2017*, edited by Robert Bird, Christina Kiaer, and Zachary Cahill, Milan: Mousse Publishing, 2017. Entry for April 9. Originally published in *Novyi LEF* 2, 1927, 19. Translated by Robert Bird and Christina Kiaer. See also Olga Kravets, "On Things and Comrades," *ephemera* 13: 2, 2013, 421–36.

12. McKenzie Wark likewise notes Platonov's "strikingly poignant and subtly molecular account of everyday proletarian life, among rocks, animals, and plants—as comrades." Wark, *Molecular Red*, 67.

13. Oxana Timofeeva, *History of Animals*, London: Bloomsbury, 2018, 167.

14. See also Stevphen Shukaitis, "Can the Object Be a Comrade?," *ephemera* 12: 2, 2013, 437–44.

15. Hongwei Bao, "'Queer Comrades': Transnational Popular Culture, Queer Sociality, and Socialist Legacy," *English Language Notes* 49: 1, spring/summer 2011, 131–7, at 132.

16. Ibid.

17. Jason Frank, "Promiscuous Citizenship," in *A Political Companion to Walt Whitman*, ed. John Seery, Lexington: University Press of Kentucky, 2011, 155–84, at 164.

18. Frantz Fanon, *The Wretched of the Earth*, trans. Richard Philcox, New York: Grove, 2004, 236, 239.

19. George Orwell, *Homage to Catalonia*, San Diego: Harcourt Brace, 1952, 5.

20. I am indebted to Oxana Timofeeva for this example.

21. Jean-Paul Sartre, preface to Fanon, *Wretched of the Earth*, xliii–lxii, lvi.

22. Hayden Herrera, "Frida Kahlo: Life into Art," *The Seductions of Biography*, ed. David Suchoff and Mary Rhiel, New York: Routledge, 1996, 113–7, at 115.

23. Mary Davis, *Comrade or Brother? A History of the British Labour Movement*, 2nd ed., London: Pluto, 2009, 289.

24. Platonov, *Chevengur*, 228.

25. Maria Chehonadskih uses this formulation in her dissertation, "Soviet Epistemologies and the Materialist Ontology of Poor Life."

26. Platonov, *Chevengur*, 213.

27. Ibid., 188.

28. Ibid., 326.

29. For a more complex discussion of the neighbor in its religious, sociopolitical, and mathematical meanings, see Kenneth Reinhard's entry "Neighbor," in *Dictionary of Untranslatables: A Philosophical Lexicon*, ed. Barbara Cassin, Princeton, NJ: Princeton University Press, 2015, 706–12.

30. Slavoj Žižek, *Less Than Nothing*, London: Verso, 2012, 555.

31. Ibid.

32. Bettina Aptheker, *The Morning Breaks: The Trial of Angela Davis*, New York: International Publishers, 1975, 3.

33. Jacques Derrida, *Politics of Friendship*, trans. George Collins, London: Verso, 1997, 116.

34. Claudio Lomnitz, *The Return of Comrade Ricardo Flores Magón*, New York: Zone Books, 2014, 295.

35. For a more complex account of the interconnections between friendship and comradeship in the early Soviet Union, see Sean Guillory, "We Shall Refashion Life on Earth! The Political Culture of the Young Communist League, 1918–1928," PhD diss., Department of History, University of California, Los Angeles, 2009.

36. Derrida, *Politics of Friendship*, 19.

37. Ibid., 22.

38. Wilderson, *Incognegro*, 145–6.

39. Ibid., 268.

40. Ellen Schrecker, *Many Are the Crimes*, Boston: Little, Brown, and Company, 1998, 131.

41. Ibid., 133.

42. I'm indebted to David Riff for alerting me to this point. Bartholmes, *Bruder, Bürger, Freund, Genosse und andere Wörter der sozialistischen Terminologie*, 175.

43. Jeffrey Brooks, *Thank You, Comrade Stalin! Soviet Public Culture from Revolution to Cold War*, Princeton, NJ: Princeton University Press, 2000, 24.

44. Nikolay Oleynikov and Oxana Timofeeva, "Beastly Spirits: A Pack of Folks," *Rethinking Marxism* 28: 3–4, 2016, 500–22.

45. Schrecker, *Many Are the Crimes*, 141.

46. Ibid.

47. Bertolt Brecht, *The Measures Taken and Other Lehrstücke*, eds. John Willett and Ralph Mannheim, New York: Arcade, 2001, 12.

48. Kravets, "On Things and Comrades," 422.

49. Personal communication.

50. Serguei Sakhno and Nicole Tersis, "Is a 'Friend' an 'Enemy'? Between 'Proximity' and 'Opposition,'" in *From Polysemy to Semantic Change*, ed. Martine Vanhove, 317–39, Amsterdam: John Benjamins, 2008, 334.

51. Gornick, *Romance of American Communism*, 56.

52. I am indebted to Hannah Dickinson and Kai Heron for discussions on this point.

53. Harris, *Walt Whitman and British Socialism*, 13.

54. W. Harrison Riley, "Reminiscences of Karl Marx," *Comrade* 3: 1, 1903, 5–6, at 5.

55. Bartholmes finds that by the mid-1870s, *Genosse* had become both a term of address and a designator for members of the

Social Democratic Party. Bartholmes, *Bruder, Bürger, Freund, Genosse und andere Wörter der sozialistischen Terminologie*, 183. The term had already been used in the workers movement since 1848, where it designated either all workers or workers in the same branch of industry.

56. "Marx to Dr Kugelmann concerning the Paris Commune," written April 12, 1871, Marxists Internet Archive, marxists.org.

57. For a discussion of the distinction between the formal and historical party in Marx's writing, see Gavin Walker, "The Body of Politics: On the Concept of the Party," *Theory & Event* 16: 4, 2013.

58. "Marx to Dr Kugelmann concerning the Paris Commune."

59. Karl Marx, "Instructions for the Delegates of the Provisional General Council: The Different Questions," originally published in *Der Verbote* 11 and 12, 1866, and *International Courier* 6 and 7, 1867, reissue, Marxists Internet Archive, marxists.org.

60. Alain Badiou, *Infinite Thought*, trans. Oliver Feltham and Justin Clemens, London: Continuum, 2003, 62.

61. Ibid.

62. Fidelity is but one possible reaction to the truth-event. Badiou presents two additional subjects, the reactive and the obscure. Alain Badiou, *Logic of Worlds*, trans. Alberto Toscano, London: Continuum, 2009.

63. Peter Hallward, *Badiou: A Subject to Truth*, Minneapolis: University of Minnesota Press, 2003, 129.

64. Alain Badiou, *Second Manifesto for Philosophy*, trans. Louise Burchill, Cambridge, UK: Polity, 2011, 84.

65. Alain Badiou, *The Rebirth of History*, trans. Gregory Elliott, London: Verso, 2012, 63.

66. Alain Badiou, *Theory of the Subject*, trans. Bruno Bosteels, London: Continuum, 2009, 286.

67. Ibid., 290.

68. I develop this argument in *Crowds and Party*.

69. For a more detailed critical engagement with Badiou's account

of the subject of truth, see my piece "The Subject of the Revolution," *Crisis and Critique* 4: 2, 2017, 152–73.

70. Gornick, *Romance of American Communism*, 247.

71. V. I. Lenin, "Party Discipline and the Fight against the Pro-Cadet Social Democrats," reprint, in *Lenin Collected Works*, vol. 11, Moscow: Progress, (1906) 1965, 320–3.

72. V. I. Lenin, "A Great Beginning: Heroism of the Workers in the Rear; 'Communist *Subbotniks*,'" reprint, in *Lenin's Collected Works*, vol. 29, 4th English ed., trans. George Hanna, Moscow: Progress, (1919) 1972, 409–34.

73. Ibid.

74. Orwell, *Homage to Catalonia*, 28.

75. Lenin, "A Great Beginning."

76. Gornick, *Romance of American Communism*, 197.

77. Raphael Samuel, *The Loss World of British Communism*, London: Verso, 2006, 121.

78. Zetkin, "Lenin on the *Women's Question*."

79. Liu Shaoqi, "How to Be a Good Communist," section IV, originally published 1939, reissue, Marxists Internet Archive, marxists.org.

80. Alexandra Kollontai, "Women Fighters in the Days of the Great October Revolution," reprint, in *Alexandra Kollontai: Selected Articles and Speeches*, Moscow: Progress, (1927) 1984.

81. Ibid.

82. Žižek, *Less Than Nothing*, 835.

83. Badiou, *Theory of the Subject*, 278. Revised version in Badiou, *Logic of Worlds*; discussion in Žižek's *Less Than Nothing*.

84. See my discussion in *Crowds and Party*, 182–90.

85. Badiou, *Theory of the Subject*, 291–2.

86. Ibid., 293.

87. Ibid., 290.

88. Isaac Deutscher, *The Prophet: The Life of Leon Trotsky*, London: Verso, 2015, 521.

89. Ibid., 524.

90. Ibid.
91. Žižek, *Less Than Nothing*, 834, n. 46.
92. Badiou, *Rebirth of History*, 69.
93. Deutscher, *Prophet*, 275.
94. Badiou, *Theory of the Subject*, 277–8.

Chapter Four: You Are Not My Comrade

1. Deutscher, *Prophet*, 857.
2. Ibid., 560.
3. Ibid., 906.
4. Ibid., 921.
5. Ibid., 946.
6. Naison, *Communists in Harlem during the Depression*, 47.
7. Communist Party U.S.A., *Race Hatred on Trial*, New York: Workers Library Publishers, 1931, 7.
8. Ibid.
9. Ibid., 8.
10. Ibid., italics in original.
11. Ibid. The bathroom was used for public bathing.
12. Naison, *Communists in Harlem during the Depression*, 47.
13. *Race Hatred on Trial*, 9.
14. Ibid.
15. Ibid., 11.
16. Ibid., 13.
17. Ibid., 12.
18. Ibid., 14.
19. Ibid.
20. Ibid., 16.
21. Ibid.
22. Ibid., 17.
23. Naison, *Communists in Harlem during the Depression*, 47.
24. Communist Party U.S.A., *Race Hatred on Trial*, 18.
25. Ibid., 19.

26. Ibid., 21.
27. Ibid., 27.
28. Ibid.
29. Ibid., 32.
30. Ibid.
31. Ibid.
32. Ibid., 36.
33. Ibid.
34. Ibid., 46–7.
35. "Deported for Abandoning White Chauvinism," *Daily Worker*, January 11, 1933.
36. "Defend Yokinen," *Daily Worker*, March 4, 1931.
37. "Deported for Abandoning White Chauvinism."
38. Ibid.
39. Haywood, *Black Bolshevik*, 587–8.
40. Ibid., 585.
41. Ibid., 543.
42. Ibid., 531–2.
43. Ibid., 586.
44. Ibid.
45. Ibid., 587.
46. Ibid.
47. Ibid., 588.
48. Ibid., 589.
49. Ibid.
50. Ibid.
51. Ibid., 591.
52. Ibid., 592.
53. Ibid., 594.
54. Patrick McGilligan and Paul Buhle, *Tender Comrades: A Backstory of the Hollywood Blacklist*, Minneapolis: University of Minnesota Press, 1997, 333.
55. "Moscow Trials: The Case of Bukharin; Last Plea—Evening Session, March 12," Marxists Internet Archive, marxists.org.

56. Jessica Mitford, *A Fine Old Conflict*, New York: Vintage Books, 1978, 127.

57. Gornick, *Romance of American Communism*, 176.

58. Martin Glaberman, introductory statement, in J. R. Johnson, *Marxism and the Intellectuals*, Detroit: Facing Reality Publishing Committee, 1962, 2.

59. "The Destruction of a Workers Paper: A Statement to the Editorial Board," included in *Marxism and the Intellectuals*, 20.

60. Ibid., 21.

61. Ibid., 25.

62. Griffin Fariello, *Red Scare: Memories of the American Inquisition, An Oral History*, New York: Norton, 1995, 232–3.

63. Howard Fast, *The Naked God: The Writer and the Communist Party*, New York: Frederick A. Praeger, 1957, 23.

64. Ibid., 177.

65. Howard Fast, *Being Red*, Boston: Houghton Mifflin Company, 1990.

66. "Audley Moore on Her Life in the CPUSA and Why She Resigned," YouTube video, posted by AfroMarxist, April 2, 2018, youtube.com.

67. See Erik S. McDuffie's discussion of Moore's resignation, in *Sojourning for Freedom*, 134–7.

68. Gornick, *Romance of American Communism*, 157.

69. Wilderson, *Incognegro*, 472.

70. Irving Howe, *A Margin of Hope: An Intellectual Biography*, New York: Harcourt Brace Jovanovich, 1982, 108.

71. Ibid.

72. John Earl Haynes, "Hellman and the Hollywood Inquisition: The Triumph of Spin-Control over Candor," *Film History* 10: 3, 1998, 408–14, at 412.

73. Chris Luo, "Keep Calling Each Other 'Comrade,' Chinese Communist Party Tells Members after Rule Review," *South China Morning Post*, November 18, 2014.

74. Moshe Levin, *The Soviet Century*, London: Verso, 2016, 41.
75. "I Am Tired, Comrades," *Pall Mall Gazette*, September 17, 1921.
76. Harvey Matusow, *False Witness*, New York: Cameron & Kahn, 1955.
77. Elizabeth Bentley, *Out of Bondage*, New York: Devin-Adair, 1951; Kathryn S. Olmsted, *Red Spy Queen: A Biography of Elizabeth Bentley*, Chapel Hill: University of North Carolina Press, 2002.
78. Doris Lessing, *The Golden Notebook*, New York: Simon and Schuster, 1962, xi.
79. Ibid., 223.
80. Ibid., 21.
81. Ibid., 24.
82. Ibid.
83. Ibid.
84. Ibid., 48.
85. Ibid., 136.
86. Ibid., 51.
87. Ibid., 136.
88. Ibid.
89. Ibid.
90. Ibid.
91. Ibid., 204.
92. Ibid., 223.
93. Ibid.
94. Ibid., 234.
95. Ibid., 255.
96. Ibid., 258.
97. Ibid.
98. Ibid.
99. Ibid.
100. Ibid., 259.
101. Ibid., 293.

102. Ibid.
103. Ibid., 301.
104. Ibid., 296, 297.
105. Ibid., 298.
106. Ibid., 299.
107. Ibid., 307.
108. Ibid., 301.
109. Ibid., 323.
110. Ibid.
111. Ibid.
112. Ibid., 407.
113. Ibid., 475.
114. Ibid., 504.
115. Ibid., 533.
116. Ibid.
117. Ibid., 537.
118. Ibid.
119. Ibid., 538.
120. Ibid., 555.
121. Ibid., 567.